Spectrum of English GOLD

Language

Composition

Dramatic Expression

Albert R. Kitzhaber
Annabel R. Kitzhaber
Edna P. DeHaven
Barbara T. Salisbury
Daisy M. Jones

Glencoe Publishing Co., Inc.
Encino, California

Acknowledgments

Field Enterprises Educational Corporation. Excerpt from an article on Marian Anderson by Daniel A. Harris and an article on Mark Twain by John C. Gerber. The World Book Encyclopedia, Vols. 1 & 19. Copyright © 1977 by Field Enterprises Educational Corporation.

Photography

Albert Bendelius from Van Cleve Photography 221

Marshall Berman, Jr. 53, 64 left, 65, 68, 112

Culver Pictures 274

Elizabeth Crews, Cover, 28, 53 right, 254, 257, 282, 283, 286

Randolph Falk 78, 79

Nebraska State Historical Society 277

Nick Pavloff 22, 23, 31, 53 left, 64 right, 69 top left, 106, 107, 160, 161 (courtesy of Steinhart Aquarium, California Academy of Sciences), 198-199, 260

Bil Plummer 42, 58, 66, 69 center, right and bottom, 124, 162, 218, 230, 235

courtesy of Sea World 19

Ted Streshinsky 8, 9, 33, 53 center, 113, 134, 135, 155, 182, 183, 186, 268-269

Jane Wattenberg 36, 50-51, 240-241

Illustration

Ayxa Art
Wayne Bonnett
Ewald Breuer
David Broad
Marc Ericksen
Heather Kortebein
Pat Maloney
Norman Nicholson
Bill Shields
Ward Schumaker
Arvis Stewart
Ed Taber

Design and Production

Design Office/Bruce Kortebein Peter Martin

Glencoe Publishing Co., Inc.

17337 Ventura Boulevard
Encino, California 91316

Collier Macmillan Canada, Ltd.
Printed in the United States of America

Contents

Practice Handbook

7

1
Sentence Parts

Look at the pictures. What are some of the parts this building is being made of?

In this chapter, you review some of the things you have known about the parts that make up a sentence.

In this chapter, you will review

- three kinds of sentences
- the two main parts of a statement
- nouns and determiners in sentence subjects
- proper nouns and pronouns in sentence subjects
- verbs in sentence predicates
- nouns as direct objects
- pronouns as direct objects
- transitive and intransitive verbs
- adjectives in sentence subjects and predicates
- adverbs
- making yes/no questions
- making where-questions
- making when-questions
- making how-questions
- making who-questions
- making what-questions

Three Kinds of Sentences

Some people think that long ago there was one more continent. This continent was named Atlantis. They think that one day Atlantis sank into the sea.

Read the sentences under the picture.

Atlantis was a continent.
Why did Atlantis sink?
Tell me what you think.

- Which sentence tells something?
- Which sentence asks something?
- Which sentence tells someone to do something?

Talking Things Over

The sentences under the picture are examples of the three kinds of sentences.

A sentence that tells something is a **statement.** A statement ends with a period.

A sentence that asks something is a **question.** A question ends with a question mark.

A sentence that tells someone to do something is a **command** or **request.** A command or request ends with a period.

Read each sentence.

● Tell if it is a statement, a question, or a command.

1. Plato wrote about Atlantis.
2. When did he live?
3. Look him up in the dictionary.
4. He said Atlantis was a large island beyond the Strait of Gibraltar.
5. Where is it?
6. Look it up on a map.
7. At first, the people of Atlantis were peaceful.
8. What happened then?
9. They tried to conquer Europe and Asia.
10. The Athenians stopped them.
11. Find out who the Athenians were.
12. Atlantis disappeared in great earthquakes and floods.

Using What You Have Learned

■ Read each sentence. Then write **statement, question,** or **command** to tell what kind of sentence it is.

1. Many people have tried to find Atlantis.
2. Did it really exist?
3. Some people think it was really an island called Thera.
4. Read *20,000 Leagues under the Sea.*
5. Visit Atlantis in the submarine *Nautilus.*
6. Would you like to search for it?

■ ■ Read these sentences. Write each sentence. Begin the sentence with a capital letter. End it with the correct mark. Then write **statement, question,** or **command** to tell what kind of sentence it is.

1. everyone was waiting
2. the submarine was ready
3. be careful with those boxes
4. those things are breakable
5. where was the captain
6. finally the captain arrived
7. what was he carrying
8. look
9. the captain had a new map
10. that sunken land might be Atlantis
11. on board everyone
12. the submarine traveled for days
13. what was that ahead
14. turn on the lights
15. is that a building or just rocks
16. what is moving there
17. we can't tell
18. go find out

■ ■ ■ Write the story of what happened to the divers. In your story, use questions and commands as well as statements.

Checking Up

Finish each sentence. Write the whole sentence.

A statement is a sentence that ||||||||||||||| .
A question is a sentence that ||||||||||||||| .
A command is a sentence that ||||||||||||||| .

The Two Main Parts of a Statement

Something To Think About

Read the two parts of each statement in the boxes.

● Put the two parts of each statement together. Say each statement you make.

| The city's air | is polluted. |

| Plants | need clean air. |

| Some trees | died from air pollution. |

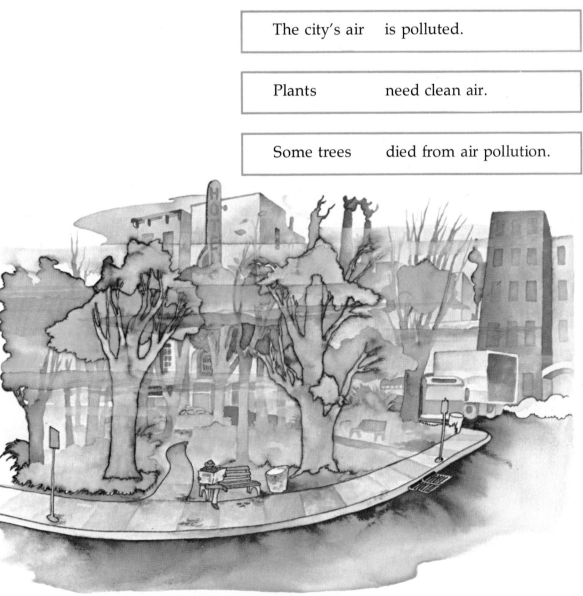

Every statement has two main parts. The first part is called the **subject.** The second part is called the **predicate.**

Read the subjects and predicates below.

• Put the subjects and predicates together to make as many sentences as you can.

Subjects	Predicates
People	litter the streets.
Animals	suffer from pollution.
Cars	create pollution.
Some industries	dump wastes into rivers.
Parks	can be kept clean.
Children	put litter in the basket.
Forest fires	are very dangerous.

Using What You Have Learned

• Join the subjects and predicates below to make four different sentences. Write each sentence you make.

	Subject	Predicate
1.	Pigeons	have wings.
2.	Penguins	cannot fly.
3.	Swans	can swim.
4.	Kangaroos	hop.
5.	Bears	sleep all winter.
6.	Our cats	are white and ginger.
7.	These dogs	can be very gentle.
8.	Sparrows	nest in the trees.
9.	Two deer	came out of the forest.
10.	Those ostriches	put their heads in the sand.

■■ Add a subject to each of these predicates. Write each statement you make.

1. |||||||||||||| are not allowed.
2. |||||||||||||| must be here at all times.
3. |||||||||||||| must turn out the lights at 8:00 P.M.
4. |||||||||||||| must be accompanied by a $5.00 fee.
5. |||||||||||||| cannot come.
6. |||||||||||||| will sing tomorrow.
7. |||||||||||||| live in caves.
8. |||||||||||||| should not be late.
9. |||||||||||||| is going to Italy.
10. |||||||||||||| built a city in the desert.

■■■ Add a predicate to each of these subjects. Write each statement you make.

1. My hair ||||||||||||||.
2. My feet ||||||||||||||.
3. My ceiling ||||||||||||||.
4. The floor ||||||||||||||.
5. Mary's cat ||||||||||||||.
6. Three giant boulders ||||||||||||||.
7. Our boats ||||||||||||||.
8. These houses ||||||||||||||.
9. The bottles ||||||||||||||.
10. Two small trees ||||||||||||||.

Checking Up

Add three different subjects to this predicate. Write the three sentences you make.

|||||||||||||| dashed into the room.

Add three different predicates to this subject. Write the three sentences you make.

Our club ||||||||||||||.

Nouns and Determiners in Sentence Subjects

Something To Think About

Giraffes bend way down to drink.
Zebras don't have this problem.
This zebra is thirsty.

Read the first sentence under the picture. The subject of each sentence is in color. The subject of the first sentence is a kind of word called a **noun.**

- Which other sentence subject is a noun alone?
- Which sentence subject is a noun with another word before it?

Talking Things Over

Sometimes the subject of a sentence is a noun alone. You can recognize many nouns by using this test sentence. Any word that fits in the blanks can be a noun.

> One whale is fine, but
> many whales are better.

Read each sentence.

- Tell what noun alone is the subject of each sentence.

1. Sauce is good with beans.
2. Cake is better with ice cream.
3. Lizards can grow new tails.
4. Birds fly.
5. Giraffes eat leaves.
6. Horses run.

Sometimes the subject of a sentence is a word such as **this** followed by a noun. **This** is called a **determiner.** The words in the box are all determiners.

a	that	three
an	those	four
the	one	some
this	two	many

Read each sentence.

- Tell what determiner is part of the subject of each sentence.
- Tell what noun follows each determiner.

1. Many hands make light work.
2. An elephant never forgets.
3. Some bread is better than none.
4. That cat has nine lives.
5. The grass is always greener on the other side of the fence.
6. Two wrongs do not make a right.
7. A stitch in time saves nine.
8. Many words mean little action.

■ The subject of each sentence below is in color. Decide what kind of word is in each subject. Then write **noun** or **determiner with noun.**

1. **A picture** is worth a thousand words.
2. **Absence** makes the heart grow fonder.
3. **Trees** grow from little acorns.
4. **Many cooks** spoil the soup.
5. **That city** was not built in a day.
6. **Money** is the root of all evil.

■ ■ Add subjects to these sentences. Use the kinds of words named in the boxes. Write the whole sentences.

1. Determiner with noun needs water.
2. Noun come out at night.
3. Determiner with noun is in the kitchen.
4. Determiner with noun is my favorite holiday.
5. Noun is made with milk.
6. Determiner with noun is strong.
7. Determiner with noun came out of the cave.
8. Noun wants to go to the museum.
9. Noun is in the attic.
10. Determiner with noun wants a piece of pie.
11. Determiner with noun falls in the summer.
12. Determiner with noun plays the guitar.

Add two different subjects to these sentences. First add a noun alone. Then add a determiner and a noun.

|||||||||||||| can fly.
|||||||||||||| tastes good.
|||||||||||||| lives in the forest.

Proper Nouns and Pronouns in Sentence Subjects

Something To Think About

Whales usually live in the ocean.
This whale lives at Sea World in San Diego.

Shamu performs many tricks.
She can leap high out of the water.
 Read the sentences above and below the picture.

- Which subject is a noun alone?
- Which subject is a determiner with a noun?
- Which sentence subject is the special name of one whale?
- Which sentence subject is a word that can be used in place of **this whale** or **Shamu?**

Talking Things Over

A sentence subject can be a noun alone. A sentence subject can be a determiner with a noun.

Sometimes the subject of a sentence is the special name of a person, a place, or a thing. Special names, such as **Shamu,** are called **proper nouns.** Each part of a proper noun begins with a capital letter.

Read these sentences.

• Tell what proper noun is the subject of each sentence.

1. James built those shelves.
2. Amanda grew that corn.
3. Jason is a carpenter.
4. Georgina is a potter.
5. Barnaby Doodle went to town.
6. Tabatha Pinkerton Rudge is my cat's name.

Sometimes the subject of a sentence is a word that can stand for nouns alone, for determiners and nouns, or for proper nouns. These words are called **pronouns.** The pronouns that can be sentence subjects are shown in the box.

Pronouns
I   you   he   she
it   we   they

Read these sentences.

• What pronoun is the subject of each sentence?

1. They danced every dance.
2. She does not believe in ghosts.
3. He belongs to every club in town.
4. It just fell into my lap.
5. You understand how I feel.
6. We never doubted you.
7. I looked everywhere for her.
8. They were very kind to them.

Using What You Have Learned

■ The subject of each sentence below is in color. Decide what kind of word is in each subject. Then write **proper noun** or **pronoun.**

1. **We** asked him to turn the radio down.
2. **Alonzo** paid for everything.
3. **Sally Super** sang.
4. **He** walked silently along the river.
5. **She** made a wish.
6. **Percy Bates** pulled in the net.
7. **They** sold the car to Alfonso.
8. **Alicia** dances in the ballet.

■ ■ Add subjects to these sentences. Use the kinds of words named in the boxes. Write the whole sentences.

1. Proper noun is my dentist.
2. Pronoun is intelligent.
3. Proper noun took care of seven dwarfs.
4. Pronoun worked very hard.
5. Proper noun lost a glass slipper.
6. Pronoun searched the kingdom for her.
7. Proper noun crosses the river at the bend.
8. Pronoun played ball all afternoon.
9. Proper noun likes her new mobile home.
10. Pronoun spilled the milk on the carpet.
11. Proper noun read about the discovery.
12. Pronoun placed the cover on the dish.

Checking Up

Add two different subjects to these sentences. First add a proper noun. Then add a pronoun.

|||||||||||||| played in the park.
|||||||||||||| helped me.
|||||||||||||| lives near me.

Verbs in Sentence Predicates

Something To Think About

They ||||||||||||| over the fence now.
Mindy ||||||||||||| over the fence now.
They ||||||||||||| over the fence yesterday.

• Use the same word to finish each sentence above the picture. Change the word so it fits each sentence. Say each sentence.

• How many different forms of the word did you use?

Talking Things Over

The word you added to each sentence is a **verb.** Every sentence predicate has a verb. Often the verb is the first word in the predicate.

Most verbs have at least three forms. Two of the forms go with **now.** They are present tense forms. One form is called the **base form.** The other is called the **-s form.** One form goes with **yesterday.** It is the **past tense form.**

Read this chart.

Verb Forms		
Present Tense Forms		Past Tense Form
Base Form	-s Form	
jump	jumps	jumped
walk	walks	walked
help	helps	helped
sew	sews	sewed
ride	rides	rode
take	takes	took
get	gets	got
talk	talks	talked
sell	sells	sold
write	writes	wrote

• How do the past tense forms of **jump, walk, help,** and **sew** end?

• What are the past tense forms of **ride, take,** and **get**?

Most past tense forms end in **-ed.** Some do not. They change differently.

Look at the sentences above the picture.

• Which **present tense** form is used in the sentence about more than one runner?

• Which **present tense** form is used in the sentence about one runner?

The **base form** is used in sentences about more than one person or thing.

The **-s form** is used in sentences about one person or thing.

- Add a different verb to complete each sentence. Use the right **present tense form.**

1. The cat |||||||||||||| under that chair.
2. Their family |||||||||||||| in the mountains.
3. They |||||||||||||| across the street.
4. He |||||||||||||| well.
5. Ringo |||||||||||||| around the park.
6. Alice |||||||||||||| carefully.

•• Add a different verb to complete each sentence. Use a **past tense form.**

1. Yesterday, Nat |||||||||||||| out of that tree.
2. Last night, I |||||||||||||| when I saw her.
3. Last year, Pam |||||||||||||| for three miles.
4. Yesterday, they |||||||||||||| to Alaska.
5. This morning, he |||||||||||||| all over the rug.
6. Last night, she |||||||||||||| for two hours.

Using What You Have Learned

■ Add a different verb to complete each sentence. Use the right **present tense form.**

1. He |||||||||||||| to school on time.
2. She |||||||||||||| dresses.
3. We |||||||||||||| many people.
4. They |||||||||||||| pancakes.
5. Marvin |||||||||||||| books at home.
6. Sarah |||||||||||||| in a store.
7. Her dog |||||||||||||| her hand.
8. They |||||||||||||| the car well.
9. Nancy |||||||||||||| detective stories.
10. The bears |||||||||||||| around the ring.
11. Herman |||||||||||||| pet hamsters.
12. The snowman |||||||||||||| in the sun.
13. The bats |||||||||||||| in the tower.
14. Parents |||||||||||||| their children.
15. The library |||||||||||||| this afternoon.

■ ■ Add a different verb to complete each sentence. Use a **past tense form.**

1. They |||||||||||||| down to the lake.
2. Bill |||||||||||||| a blue cap.
3. The moon |||||||||||||| over the rooftop.
4. The stars |||||||||||||| the sailors their way.
5. Priscilla |||||||||||||| the stairs red.
6. We |||||||||||||| the pumpkin seeds.
7. The bridge |||||||||||||| into the river.
8. Workers |||||||||||||| over the building.
9. Terry |||||||||||||| that he needs a map.
10. Cows |||||||||||||| milk.
11. Vegetables |||||||||||||| in sunny places.
12. The players |||||||||||||| the ball to Tina.
13. My mother |||||||||||||| good pies.
14. The train |||||||||||||| into the station.

Checking Up

Divide the words in the box into two groups. One group should have present tense verb forms. One group should have past tense verb forms.

drive	arrives
sell	drove
called	helped
took	walked
rang	want
wished	went
win	helps
woke	take
write	drew
takes	rode

Nouns as Direct Objects

Something To Think About

Read the sentence beginnings under the picture.

Taffy found ||||||||||||||.   He does not see ||||||||||||||.

• Add two words to finish each sentence. Say the sentences you make.

Talking Things Over

You added a **direct object** to each sentence. A direct object comes after the verb in the predicate of some sentences.

The direct object in each of these sentences is in color.

Dr. Alvarez helps **dogs.**
She helps **this dog.** •
Taffy likes **Dr. Alvarez.**

• Which direct object is a noun alone?
• Which direct object is a noun with determiner?
• Which direct object is a proper noun?

Using What You Have Learned

1. George cleans ||||||||||||||||| .
2. Abby packed ||||||||||||||| .
3. We all peeled ||||||||||||| .
4. He found ||||||||||||| .
5. Dr. West examines ||||||||||||| .

1. Jane wrote ||||||||||||||| .
2. Miguel took ||||||||||||||| .
3. We wanted ||||||||||||||| .
4. They fix ||||||||||||| .
5. Myrna called ||||||||||||| .

1. We climbed ||||||||||||| .
2. The show was called ||||||||||||||| .
3. We visited ||||||||||||| .
4. Amy likes ||||||||||||| .
5. I helped ||||||||||||| .

■ Add a direct object to each of these sentences. Use nouns in the sentences. Write the sentences.

6. Sam knows ||||||||||||||| .
7. They painted ||||||||||||||| .
8. Katy answers ||||||||||||||| .
9. I like ||||||||||||| .
10. She collects ||||||||||||| .

■ ■ Add a direct object to each of these sentences. Use only nouns with determiners. Write the sentences.

6. Tony and Janey explored ||||||||||||||| .
7. I asked ||||||||||||| .
8. Amy told ||||||||||||| .
9. The butterfly ate ||||||||||||||| .
10. The spy hid ||||||||||||| .

■ ■ ■ Add a direct object to each of these sentences. Use only proper nouns. Write the sentences.

6. She saw ||||||||||||| .
7. Milt drove ||||||||||||| home.
8. The street is named ||||||||||||||| .
9. My name is ||||||||||||| .
10. He amuses ||||||||||||| .

Checking Up

Finish this sentence three times. Add a noun alone, a noun with determiner, and a proper noun to the sentence. Write the three sentences you make.

I like ||||||||||||||| .

Pronouns as Direct Objects

Something To Think About   Read the sentences under the picture. A pronoun is part of each sentence.

- In which sentences is a pronoun the subject?
- In which sentences is a pronoun the direct object?

I helped Tanya.
Tanya helped me.

We helped José.
José helped us.

He helped Adele.
Adele helped him.

She helped Larry.
Larry helped her.

They helped George.
George helped them.

You helped Helen.
Helen helped you.

28

Talking Things Over

Pronouns can be used like determiners and nouns and like proper nouns. **Pronouns can follow verbs as direct objects** in sentences.

Read the first pair of sentences again.

- What is the pronoun in the first sentence?
- What is the pronoun in the second sentence?

I and **me** both stand for the same person. These words are two forms of the same pronoun. Use the **I** form as the subject. Use the **me** form as the direct object.

Read the other pairs of sentences under the picture. Answer these questions about each pair.

- What form of the pronoun is used as the subject?
- What form of the pronoun is used as the object?

I, he, she, we, they, it, and **you** are used as subjects.

Me, him, her, us, them, it, and **you** are used as direct objects.

- What pronoun is the direct object in each of these sentences?

1. Ted found it.
2. I telephoned them.
3. Geraldine told him.
4. She will tell you.

5. Cory asked me.
6. The dog frightened her.
7. That sound surprised us.
8. That bus took them.

- Use a pronoun as a direct object in each sentence.

1. Our dog chewed |||||||||||||||.
2. Donna and I visited |||||||||||||||.
3. Aunt Nora greeted |||||||||||||||.

4. Several people knew |||||||||||||||.
5. The storm delayed |||||||||||||||.
6. The walk tired |||||||||||||||.

■ Each of these sentences has a pronoun as the direct object. Write the direct object from each sentence.

1. Coretta chose them.
2. Jenny heard us.
3. Gordon fixed it.
4. My sister visited her.
5. The doctor examined me.
6. The kitten liked you.

■■ The direct object in each sentence is a proper noun or a noun with determiner. Change the direct object to a pronoun. Write each of the sentences.

1. We visited the museum.
2. Norman saw Dr. Alvarez.
3. Dana watered the plants.
4. We heard Lupe and Roger.
5. The question puzzled James.
6. Many people helped Cloris.
7. Mr. Lee taught Kathy and Rodrigo.
8. That answer annoyed Ted.
9. The teacher asked Gina.
10. The player dropped the ball.
11. Miss Loring bought these dishes.
12. Mike packed the books.
13. Lisa showed Tanya and Don.
14. Carla wound the clock.
15. The bear grabbed the salmon.
16. Paul watered those plants.

Checking Up

Write three sentences. Use a different pronoun as a direct object in each one.

Transitive and Intransitive Verbs

Something To Think About

Read the sentences under the picture.

- What is the verb in each sentence?
- Which sentences have direct objects after the verbs?
- Which sentences do not have direct objects after the verbs?

Sasha **told** a joke.　　Carl **clapped** his hands.
Everyone **listened.**　　Lee **asked** a riddle.
Dana **laughed.**　　　　Jerry **guessed.**

31

Talking Things Over

A verb that is followed by a direct object is a **transitive** verb. A verb that is not followed by a direct object is an **intransitive verb.**

Read the sentences under the picture again.

- Which verbs are transitive?
- Which verbs are intransitive?
- Find the verb in each sentence below. Tell whether it is transitive or intransitive.

1. The store sold pies.
2. We wanted candy.
3. He smiled.
4. She laughed.
5. Nellie found the pig.
6. The pig blinked.

7. Steve opened the cans.
8. Rachel heated the soup.
9. They planted turnips.
10. Amelia dances.
11. We stopped.
12. They listened.

Using What You Have Learned

■ Find the verb in each sentence. Write **transitive** if the verb is followed by a direct object. Then write the direct object from the sentence. Write **intransitive** if the verb is not followed by a direct object.

1. She strung the beads.
2. He watched.
3. They waited.
4. He rocked the boat.
5. Tom pinched the cat.
6. The cat scratched Tom.
7. The dogs barked.
8. The wolves howled.

9. The storm raged.
10. Sue closed the windows.
11. The windows rattled.
12. The radio played music.
13. Everyone listened.
14. We ate cookies.
15. Jana read a magazine.
16. The kitten slept.

Checking Up

Write two sentences that have transitive verbs. Write two sentences that have intransitive verbs.

Adjectives in Sentence Subjects and Predicates

Something To Think About

Many buildings are **tall.**
These people are working on a **tall** building.
The **tall** building will have many offices.

Read the sentences under the picture. The word **tall** is in all three sentences.

- In which sentences is **tall** part of the predicate?
- In which sentence is **tall** part of the subject?

33

Talking Things Over

Tall is an adjective. You can check by putting **tall** in the test sentence for adjectives.

> It is very tall .

Adjectives can be in both parts of statements. Adjectives can be in the subjects of statements. They can come before nouns in sentence subjects. Adjectives can also be in the predicates of statements. They can come before nouns in sentence predicates. They can follow forms of **be** as completers.

Each sentence below has one adjective.

- In which sentences is the adjective part of the predicate?
- In which sentences is the adjective part of the subject?

1. The clown was funny.
2. A blue wig sat on his head.
3. He was wearing green teeth.
4. His shoes were enormous.
5. A floppy hat covered his wig.
6. His baggy pants were held up by rope.

Each sentence below has two adjectives.

- What adjective is in the subject of each statement?
- What adjective is in the predicate of each statement?

1. The wet boots left dirty marks.
2. The silent room seemed unfriendly.
3. Her red scarf is on that low table.
4. The huge elephant ate a little peanut.
5. The excited girl pushed open the heavy door.

■ Each sentence below has two adjectives. Write each adjective. Next to the adjective write whether it is in the subject or the predicate.

1. The small apples are ripe.
2. The old woman was friendly.
3. Those deep puddles are dangerous.
4. The frightened animal hid in the dark cave.
5. A beautiful garden is behind that old house.
6. A heavy box is on that shaky table.
7. A bright meteor crossed the dark sky.
8. My little sister baked a chocolate cake.
9. The first contestant was bright.
10. The young panda was playful.

■■ Add an adjective to each sentence. Write the sentence.

1. Mickey is |||||||||||||||| .
2. A |||||||||||||||| girl helped us.
3. The monster was |||||||||||||||| .
4. A |||||||||||||||| ghost haunts this house.
5. Her hair is |||||||||||||||| .
6. A |||||||||||||||| kitten hid behind the chair.
7. The bags are |||||||||||||||| .
8. Two |||||||||||||||| boxes are on the shelf.
9. A |||||||||||||||| vampire stood at the window.
10. The sound was |||||||||||||||| .

Checking Up

Write each sentence three times. Use a different adjective each time.

The |||||||||||||||| bird sang.
The song was |||||||||||||||| .

35

Adverbs

Read the sentences under the picture.

The package arrived **here.**
The package arrived **today.**
The package arrived **safely.**

- Which sentence tells where the package arrived?
- Which word in that sentence tells where?
- Which sentence tells when the package arrived?
- Which word in that sentence tells when?
- Which sentence tells how the package arrived?
- Which word in that sentence tells how?

Talking Things Over

Words such as **here, today,** and **safely** are called **adverbs.**

Adverbs such as **here** tell **where.**

● Find the adverb that tells **where** in each sentence.

1. The macaroni is there.
2. Your watch is upstairs.
3. The snow fell everywhere.
4. I can't find my gloves anywhere.
5. Bring the plant inside.
6. Place your forks here.
7. What is in the room above?
8. I must go below.

Adverbs such as **today** tell **when.**

● Find the adverb that tells **when** in each sentence.

1. I'll think about it tomorrow.
2. Should we go tonight?
3. I caught a polliwog yesterday.
4. Dessert will be ready soon.
5. The boys are going now.
6. Bring me the book early.
7. Will you come back today?
8. She came in late.

Adverbs such as **safely** tell **how.**

● Find the adverb that tells **how** in each sentence.

1. The time went by quickly.
2. The gull swooped down gracefully.
3. He looked around thoughtfully.
4. The tiger crept up silently.
5. She introduced me warmly.
6. The tiger jumped swiftly.

Using What You Have Learned

■ Find the adverb in each sentence. Write that word. Then write **where, when,** or **how** to show what the adverb tells.

1. The baby crawled upstairs.
2. She smiled weakly.
3. I can hear it now.
4. Phil put his cup down.
5. Let's find that pony tonight.
6. Angela hid the ribbon quickly.
7. It is hidden below.
8. She is out.
9. I can see it dimly.
10. Do not visit the castle tomorrow.
11. The fog drifted in slowly.
12. Use your pencils carefully.

■■ Write each sentence three times. First add an adverb that tells **where.** Next add an adverb that tells **when.** Then add an adverb that tells **how.** If you want, choose adverbs from the boxes.

Where		When		How	
here	outside	yesterday	soon	patiently	happily
outdoors	upstairs	early	late	busily	noisily
there	somewhere	today	now	quickly	carefully
inside	downstairs	tomorrow	then	suddenly	quietly

1. I want to write it ||||||||||||||||.
2. She took the onions ||||||||||||||||.
3. He walked ||||||||||||||||.
4. They waited for you ||||||||||||||||.
5. He threw his cap off ||||||||||||||||.
6. She hit the ball ||||||||||||||||.
7. Place it ||||||||||||||||.
8. She dresses ||||||||||||||||.
9. I ran ||||||||||||||||.
10. I have to wake up ||||||||||||||||.
11. Paula hid the locket ||||||||||||||||.
12. Hurry ||||||||||||||||.
13. We will see her ||||||||||||||||.
14. The ghost came down the stairs ||||||||||||||||.

Checking Up

An adverb can tell |||||||||||||||| something happens.
An adverb can tell |||||||||||||||| something happens.
An adverb can tell |||||||||||||||| something happens.

Making Yes/No Questions

Read the sentences under the first picture.

The Jumbliks **have** lost something.
Have the Jumbliks lost something?

They **can** find it.
Can they find it?

The Jumblik found his sock.
Did the Jumblik find his sock?

The room looks worse than ever.
Does the room look worse than ever?

The Jumbliks try to make it neater.
Do the Jumbliks try to make it neater?

- How was the order of the words in each statement changed to make a question?

  Read the sentences under the second picture.

- What was added to each statement to make a question?

- What words in the first two statements were changed in the questions?

The questions on page 39 can be answered **yes** or **no.** Questions such as these are called **yes/no questions.**

You can use the words in many statements to make yes/no questions. You only have to change the order of the words.

• Change the order of the words in each of these statements to make a yes/no question.

1. The room is a mess.
2. The Jumbliks will fix it.
3. The Jumbliks should hurry.
4. They would like to go out.
5. They can finish in time.
6. They are ready now.
7. They will have to wait.
8. The Jumbliks are sad.

Sometimes you have to add something to the words of a statement to make a yes/no question. You can add **do, does,** or **did** to make a yes/no question. You may also have to change the form of the verb in the statement.

• Use the words in each statement to make a yes/no question. Begin each question with **do, does,** or **did.** Change any other word that needs to be changed.

1. He feels bad.
2. He lost his new sock.
3. His aunt made them.
4. She knits well.
5. They feel good.
6. They fit perfectly.
7. The train got in on time.
8. Our team won all the medals.

Using What You Have Learned

■ Change the order of the words in each statement to make a yes/no question. Write the yes/no question.

1. The party will start at five.
2. We could bake a cake.
3. We should buy a pie.
4. They can float the boat.
5. He will try to fly.
6. We were high in the sky.
7. Terry was late for the movies.
8. The children would like to sing.
9. Their boats were in the water.
10. Your father was in the army.

■■ Use the words in each statement to make a yes/no question. Begin each question with **do, does,** or **did.** If you need to, change one of the words in the statement.

1. She presses her dress.
2. He washes squash.
3. They like the bike.
4. She flies faster than Fred.
5. They weigh trays.
6. She eats meat.
7. The runners ran around the park.
8. Our school won the prize.
9. Mary likes to ride buses.
10. The magazine has one hundred pages.

Checking Up

Write three yes/no questions of your own.

Then write a statement to answer each yes/no question.

Making Where-Questions, When-Questions, and How-Questions

Read the sentences under the picture.

Where can the bison graze?
The bison can graze **here.**

When can the bison graze?
The bison can graze **now.**

How can the bison graze?
The bison can graze **safely.**

- Which sentence asks where the bison can graze?
- Which sentence tells where the bison can graze?
- Which sentence asks when the bison can graze?
- Which sentence tells when the bison can graze?
- Which sentence asks how the bison can graze?
- Which sentence tells how the bison can graze?

Talking Things Over

Sentences that ask **where** are called **where-questions.** A where-question can be answered by a statement with an adverb that tells where.

● What **where-question** can be answered by each of these statements?

1. The ducks went away.
2. She met him downstairs.
3. He crawled outside.
4. They found her there.
5. They searched everywhere.

Sentences that ask **when** are called **when-questions.** A when-question can be answered by a statement with an adverb that tells when.

● What **when-question** can be answered by each of these statements?

1. The races will start soon.
2. These tracks were made yesterday.
3. She left early.
4. The dance will end early.
5. He will put the cat out tonight.
6. They are making the soup now.

Sentences that ask **how** are called **how-questions.** A how-question can be answered by a statement with an adverb that tells how.

● What **how-question** can be answered by each of these statements?

1. He knocked on the door sharply.
2. The students sat up quickly.
3. They closed their eyes thoughtfully.
4. He gave the orders quickly.
5. The children answered loudly.
6. Mr. Ortez sang softly.

■ Write a statement to answer each of these questions. Use an adverb from the box in each statement.

soon	now
outdoors	inside
downstairs	here
badly	early
yesterday	today
tomorrow	softly
late	well
quietly	gracefully
quickly	carefully

1. Where did you hide the teapot?
2. How will you wake her?
3. When will you tell them?
4. Where did they run?
5. How does he skate?
6. When will the band play?
7. When will they come?
8. How are they dressed?
9. Where have they kept it?
10. How are they feeling?
11. When can she go?
12. Where does it live?
13. When will it stop?
14. How did it look?
15. Where can we go?

■■ Write the where-question, when-question, or how-question that can be answered by each statement below.

1. He received the note yesterday.
2. He read it carefully.
3. He walked there.
4. She was waiting for him outside.
5. He will race tomorrow.
6. He shouted joyfully.

Checking Up

Write a when-question, a where-question, and a how-question. Then write statements to answer each question. Use one word from the box in each statement.

Making Who-Questions and What-Questions

Read the sentences under the picture.

Who found our puppy?
Pia found our puppy.

What had hidden the puppy?
The pine tree had hidden the puppy.

What was the puppy chewing?
The puppy was chewing **a pine cone.**

- Which sentence asks who found the puppy?
- Which sentence tells who found the puppy?
- Which sentence asks what had hidden the puppy?
- Which sentence tells what had hidden the puppy?
- Which sentence asks what the puppy was chewing?
- Which sentence tells what the puppy was chewing?

Questions that ask **who** are called **who-questions.** Most who-questions can be answered by a statement that names a person.

• What who-question can be answered by each of these statements?

1. A visitor was in the room.
2. Someone was eating honey.
3. Nikki was in the garden.
4. Jack Horner became a baker.
5. An old woman lived in the old house.
6. Tony sat near the window.

Questions that ask **what** are called **what-questions.** Most what-questions can be answered by a statement that names a thing or a place.

• What what-question can be answered by each of these statements?

1. He saw spots.
2. She gave him some soup.
3. Snow covered the steps.
4. He looked for the shovel.
5. She threw salt on the steps.

Using What You Have Learned

■ Write a statement to answer each of these questions. Name a person in your answer to each **who-question.**

1. Who wants to go to the beach?
2. Who is in that room?
3. Who will come?
4. Who wears jeans?
5. Who goes up the ladder?
6. Who has a new bike?

■ ■ Write a statement to answer each of these questions. Name a place or thing in your answer to each **what-question.**

1. What climbed up the rope?
2. What will you wear to the party?
3. What goes up the chimney?
4. What have you got in that bag?
5. What way will you go to get there?
6. What is your favorite dessert?

■ ■ ■ Write the **who-question** or **what-question** that can be answered by each statement below.

1. Joan won't believe this.
2. A lizard was in the lettuce.
3. John found it.
4. Judy caught it.
5. It ate lettuce and squash.
6. It liked to sit in the sun.
7. Fred took the lizard for walks.
8. Nancy made it a little collar.
9. It enjoyed the walks.
10. Lizards like to exercise.

Checking Up

Write two who-questions and two what-questions. Write a statement that answers each question.

47

Choosing the Right Present Tense Verb Form

My friend **likes** the airport.
She **watches** every plane.
That plane **lands** quickly.

My friends **like** the airport.
They **watch** every plane.
Those planes **land** quickly.

Read the sentences in the blue box. Each sentence
is about one person or thing. The subject of each
sentence is singular.

- What is the verb in each sentence?
- How do verbs that go with singular subjects end?

Read the sentences in the red box. Each sentence
is about more than one person or thing. The subject
of each sentence is plural.

- What is the verb in each sentence?
- How do verbs that go with plural subjects end?

For Practice

■ Choose the verb form that goes with the subject
of each sentence. Write the sentence.

1. The game start, starts late.
2. The fans wait, waits impatiently.
3. The players run, runs onto the field.
4. An official blow, blows the whistle.
5. One player kick, kicks the ball.
6. Three other players chase, chases it.
7. They all bump, bumps into each other.
8. A fourth player catch, catches the ball.
9. The fans cheer, cheers loudly.
10. One fan wave, waves a banner.
11. The cheerleaders lead, leads the cheering.
12. One cheerleader turn, turns a somersault.

Remember

Present tense verbs have two
different forms.

One form goes with singular
subjects. This form ends with
s. It is called the -s form.
Smiles, laughs, and talks are -s
form verbs.

The other form goes with
plural subjects. It is called the
base form. Smile, laugh, and
talk are base form verbs.

◆ If you need more help,
turn to pages 38 and 40 of
your Practice Handbook.

More about Choosing the Right Verb Form

> The cat **looks** scared.
> The cat in that tree **looks** scared.

> The cats **look** scared.
> The cats in that tree **look** scared.

Read the sentences in the blue box. Each sentence is about one cat.

- What is the verb in each sentence?
- How does adding **in that tree** change the verb form?

Read the sentences in the red box. Each sentence is about more than one cat.

- What is the verb in each sentence?
- How does adding **in that tree** change the verb form?

For Practice

■ Write the second sentence in each pair. Choose the right verb form from the box.

1. The stores are not open yet.
   The stores in that center is, are not open yet.
2. The books belong to Margo.
   The books over there belongs, belong to Margo.
3. Soft corals have eight tentacles.
   Soft corals such as this sea fan has, have eight tentacles.
4. Those stories sound interesting.
   The stories about it sounds, sound scary.
5. Both bridges look unsafe.
   Both bridges across this river looks, look unsafe.

■ ■ Write each sentence. Choose the right verb form from the box.

1. The campground up the river is, are for canoeists.
2. A trip in a canoe takes, take a lot of planning.
3. Packs in the canoe gets, get wet sometimes.
4. The paddlers in a canoe needs, need cushions.
5. Some canoes on this lake has, have sails.

- If you need more help, turn to pages 38 and 40 of your Practice Handbook.

2

Writing Details and Descriptions

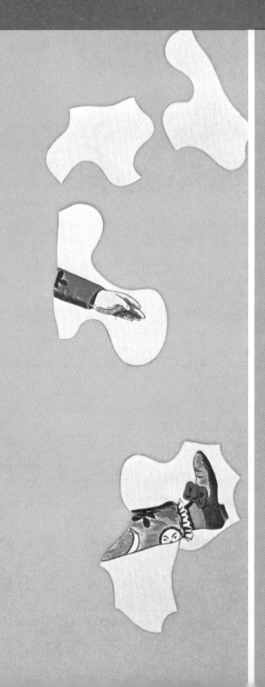

Look at the puzzle. Each piece contains a detail. If you put the pieces together you will have a complete figure. In this chapter, you will learn more about how details can help you describe people and places more clearly.

In this chapter, you will

- write details about a person
- use these details to write a description
- describe a trip
- describe a perfect day

Writing Details about a Person

Look at the picture of Martin.

- What is the main idea that this picture gives about Martin? Certain details helped to give you that idea. Look at the picture again.
- Where is Martin?
- What does the way Martin is sitting tell you about him?
- What other things do you notice about Martin?

Talking about Your Ideas

Look at each picture on the next page.

- What is the main idea that the picture gives you about the person?
- Where is the person?
- What does the way the person is sitting, standing, or moving tell you about the person?
- What other things do you notice about the person?

Writing about Your Ideas

■ Think about someone you know. Picture that person in a certain place, doing something. Write your answers to these questions.

1. What is the main idea that the picture in your mind gives you about the person?
2. Where is the person?
3. What does the way the person is sitting, standing, or moving tell you about the person?
4. What other things do you notice about the person?

Checking Up

Read your answers. Decide which two helped most to give you your main idea of the person. Draw a line under those answers.

Writing a Description of a Person

Looking for Ideas

Lael is writing a description of Martin.

- What is she using to help her?

Talking about Your Ideas

Lael answered the questions on the top of page 52. Read them again. Then read Lael's answers.

> 1. Martin is completely lost in his book.
> 2. He is sitting under a tree in the park.
> 3. The way he sits shows how relaxed he is.
> 4. Martin doesn't notice the puppy.

54

Now read Lael's description.

Martin

Martin is a person who can **lose himself in a book.** Here he is **in the park.** It is one of his favorite places. **The way he sits shows how relaxed he is** as he sits **under the tree.** Martin is too interested in his book to notice anything else. He **doesn't** even **notice the puppy,** who would like to play.

The words in color come from Lael's answers to the questions. She added the other details.

- What details did Lael add?

Writing about Your Ideas

■ In the last lesson, you answered the same questions Lael did. You can use the answers to write a description. Write your description the way Lael did.

Begin by giving the main idea.
—What is the main idea?
Put in the answers to the other questions.
—What are the answers?
Add any details that will give a clearer picture.
—What details will you add?

Checking Up

Read your paragraph.
Draw lines under the words that come from your answers to the questions.

Describing a Trip

Marina is thinking of all the places she would like to visit.

- What real places does Marina want to visit? What do these places look like?
- What imaginary place does she want to visit? What does this place look like?
- Whom does she want to take along on two of the trips?
- What would she do in each place?

56

Talking about Your Ideas

Imagine you can go anywhere you like. Think of the places you might visit.

- What real place would you like to visit?
- What imaginary place would you like to visit? What would this place be like?

Think of what might happen in each place you visit.

- What would you like to see?
- What would you like to do?
- Whom would you like to have there with you?
- How long would you like to stay?

Writing about Your Ideas

■ Choose one place you would like to visit. You may choose a real place. You may make up a place.

Write a paragraph about your trip. You may want to use this beginning for your paragraph:

I am going on a trip to ||||||||||||||.

In the rest of your paragraph, answer these questions:

—What will the place be like?
—Who will be with you?
—What will you do there?
—How long will you stay?

Checking Up

Read your paragraph.
Draw a line under the sentences that tell what the place is like.
Circle the sentences that tell what you will do.

Describing a Perfect Day

Looking for Ideas

Donna thought about the things she most likes to do. Then she planned a perfect day for herself.

- What did Donna plan to do in the morning?
- What did she plan to do in the afternoon?
- What did she plan to do in the evening?

Morning   Afternoon   Evening

Talking about Your Ideas

Imagine you are planning your own perfect day. You can do anything you want all day long.

Think about the things you might do on the morning of your perfect day.

- What would you choose to do?
- Where would you like to do it?
- With whom would you like to do it?

Think of the things you might do during the afternoon and evening.

- What would you choose to do?
- Where would you like to do it?
- With whom would you like to do it?

Writing about Your Ideas

■ Make up a plan for your own perfect day. Write three paragraphs about the day you plan.

In the first paragraph, tell what you would do on the morning of your perfect day. Tell where you would do it. Tell with whom you would do it.

In the second paragraph, tell what you would do during the afternoon of your perfect day. Tell where you would do it. Tell with whom you would do it.

In the third paragraph, tell what you would do in the evening of your perfect day. Tell where you would do it. Tell with whom you would do it.

You may want to use these sentence beginnings to start your paragraphs.

On the morning of my perfect day, I would ||||||||||||||||||||||||||||||||||||||||||||||||||||||||||||||||||||||||||||||||||||||||||||||||||| .

During the afternoon of my perfect day, I would ||||||||||||||||||||||||||||||||||||||||||||||||||||||||||||||||||||||||||||||||||||||||||||||| .

In the evening of my perfect day, I would ||||||||||||||||||||||||||||||||||||||||||||||||||||||||||||||||||||||||||||||||||||||||||||||||| .

Checking Up

What activity did you tell about in each of your paragraphs?

Using Capital Letters

> Who gave **P**aula **S**lominski the kitten?
> **S**he named her kitten **F**endo.
> **L**ake **T**emescal is in **O**akland, **C**alifornia.
> **R**oberto gave a report about schools in **J**apan.
> **T**hanksgiving is the third **T**hursday in **N**ovember.
> **H**ave you read *A Billion for Boris*?

Read the sentences in the box. Notice each capital letter.

• How does the first word in every sentence begin?

• How does each part of a person's name or a pet's name begin?

• How does each part of the name of a place, a city, a state, or a country begin?

• How does each part of the name of a holiday, a day of the week, or a month of the year begin?

• How do the first word and every important word in a title begin?

For Practice

▪ Write these sentences. Add capital letters wherever they are needed.

1. My friend maurice lives in madison, wisconsin.
2. Dad and mr. crosby climbed mount whitney.
3. we had a party on halloween.
4. connie and i are reading *walk the world's rim.*
5. we moved from south carolina to south dakota.
6. melissa named the parakeets pinta and nina.
7. this ship sails from california to alaska.
8. They hiked from buckskin ridge to lake tandy.
9. Rich Klein and bonnie Brodski play in the band.
10. we can go to the movie on tuesday, thursday, or saturday.
11. rhonda, les, and carrie all have birthdays in april.
12. have you read *The walking stones?*

Remember

A word begins with a capital letter if it is

—the first word in a sentence
—the name of a person or pet
—the name of a place, a city, a state, or a country
—the name of a holiday, a day of the week, or a month of the year
—the first word or an important word in a title

• If you need more help, turn to pages 1–5 of your Practice Handbook.

Writing Titles of Stories and Books

> My favorite story is "Past the Fifth Galaxy."
> It is in <u>Reach for the Stars</u>, a book of
> science fiction stories.

Read the sentences in the box.

- What mark comes at the beginning and the end of the title of a story?
- What mark comes under each word in the title of a book?

For Practice

■ Write these sentences about stories. Add quotation marks at the beginning and the end of the title of each story.

1. Last Chance for Chauncey was a funny story.
2. We read Off the Deep End yesterday.
3. Now or Never was written by Lonny Lorenz.
4. One of Janey's favorite stories is The Greatest Ghost.
5. I liked The Greedy Goblin.
6. Mom used to read us a story called Bread and Jam.

■■ Write these sentences about books. Underline the title of each book.

1. Maureen is reading Cameras and Courage.
2. Our class read Ishii in Two Worlds.
3. Brad read some poems from I Am the Darker Brother.
4. Spare Parts for the Human Body is an interesting book.
5. Have you read Pie in the Sky?
6. I liked Zooming In.

Remember

Quotation marks come at the beginning and the end of the title of a story.

Each word in the title of a book is underlined.

- If you need more help, turn to page 18 of your Practice Handbook.

Using End Punctuation

Statement:	Plankton are plants and animals that drift through water.
Question:	Are all plankton tiny?
Command:	Look through this microscope.
Sentences That Show Strong Feeling:	I can see the plankton moving! Watch them!

Read the sentences in the box. Notice the punctuation mark at the end of each sentence.

• How does a statement end?
• How does a question end?
• How does a command end?
• How does a sentence that shows strong feeling end?

For Practice

■ Write these sentences. Add a period, a question mark, or an exclamation mark at the end of each sentence.

1. Have you ever seen a bear roller-skate
2. That sounds impossible
3. Trainers can teach wild animals many tricks
4. Animal trainers need a lot of patience
5. Watch that monkey on the swing
6. The monkey is turning flips
7. Look out
8. Did the monkey hit you
9. Ten tigers formed a pyramid
10. Which tiger is on top

Remember

Every sentence ends with a punctuation mark.

A statement ends with a period.

A question ends with a question mark.

A command ends with a period.

A statement or a command that shows strong feelings ends with an exclamation mark.

• If you need more help, turn to page 6 of your Practice Handbook.

Proofreading for Capital Letters and Punctuation Marks

> A
> ~~a~~n athlete may get athlete's foot.
> C
> ~~c~~an an astronaut get missile toe ?

Read the sentences in the box. The writing in red shows how you can make changes in your writing.

- How can you change a small letter to a capital letter?
- How can you add a punctuation mark?

For Practice

■ Write these sentences. Add capital letters, periods, and question marks wherever they are needed.

1. Where does benny think fish come from
2. he thinks they all come from Finland.
3. what is the difference between here and there?
4. The only difference is the letter *t*
5. what has 88 keys but can't unlock a single door
6. That sounds like a piano
7. what do you and a pin have in common?
8. we both have heads
9. we're also both pretty sharp
10. What can you hold in your left hand but not in your right
11. that must be my right elbow
12. It could also be my right wrist
13. what has four legs but can't walk
14. maybe that's a table
15. are you sure

3
Moving in Many Ways

Look at the pictures. The people in each picture are pantomiming an action. What do you think the action is in each picture?

In this chapter, you will learn more about how to use movement to show what is happening.

In this chapter, you will learn how to

- react to movement
- freeze movement
- move in slow motion
- act with objects

Reacting to Movement

Imagine you are standing in a circle like this one.

• The ball is coming to you from your left. You catch it. Now throw it to the person on your right.

• The ball is coming around again. This time the boys and girls are passing it behind them. Catch the ball on your left. Throw it to the person on your right.

• The ball is being passed over everyone's head. Catch it on your right. Throw it to the person on your left.

• Now five balls are being thrown across the circle. Here comes a high one. It is almost too high. Reach way up. You've caught it! Throw it to the person across from you.

- A low ball is coming from across the circle to the left. Catch it and throw it back.

- The balls are coming faster and faster. Keep catching and returning them.

Working It Out

When you act with someone, you must pay careful attention to what that person says and does. When you do so, then you know how to **react.**

- Work with a friend. Imagine you are throwing a basketball to each other. This is a special ball. You can make it very light. Just say "light" when you throw the ball. Your friend must catch and throw a light ball.

You can also make the ball very heavy. Just say "heavy" when you throw the ball to your friend. Your friend must catch and throw back a heavy ball.

- Throw the ball to your friend. Say whether it is light or heavy. Tell your friend what to do with the ball. You might tell your friend to do one of these things:

—bounce the ball
—dribble the ball
—hide the ball
—shoot a basket
—do anything else with the ball

- Now your friend will throw the ball to you. Listen to whether the ball is heavy or light and what you are to do with it.

Acting It Out

■ Work with four or five friends. Take turns being the leader. Have the leader stand a few feet away from the group.

The leader should think of a group of simple movements. The leader might say, "Lift both arms above your head. Bend down and touch your ankles. Then show that you are tired."

The leader then shows the same movements. Finally the group does the movements.

■■ Work with the same group. Take turns being the leader. This time the leader must describe and then do some real action. The leader might say, "Reach up to the cabinet. Open its door. Take out a cup. Put the cup on the table. Open the refrigerator. Take out the milk. Open the container. Pour the milk into the cup. Put the container back in the refrigerator. Pick up the cup. Drink the milk."

The group then does the same action.

Talking It Over

Think about the different actions. Which actions were easiest to do? Why do you think so?

Freeze Frame and Slow Motion

Look at the photographs. Each shows a fraction of a second in an action that took longer.

• What does each photo show?

Imagine you are in a movie about yourself. Every so often the movie stops. A still picture of you is frozen on the screen.

• You look at the pitcher. You see him throw the ball. You start to hit the ball.

• You are playing basketball. You are dribbling the ball across the court. Freeze! Notice how you are standing.

• You are in front of the basket. You want to shoot. The other team is blocking you. You think you can make it. You shoot. Freeze! Notice how you are jumping.

Working It Out

Every movement is made of many smaller movements.

Imagine you are in a movie again. This time the movie is in slow motion.

- You are walking up stairs.
- You are running for your bus.
- You are trying to get through a crowd.
- Work with a friend. You are laying a floor. You and your friend go over to a pile of planks. You pick one up together. You carry it to the floor. You lay it in place. You both nail it down. Then you do the same thing again.

Acting It Out

You can act out a play in slow motion.
- Work with a friend. You two have a job to do. Decide what the job is. You have a problem in doing this job. Decide what the problem is. It might be

—something that is missing
—someone who tries to stop you
—the weather
—anything else

Plan how you will solve the problem.

Make up your play. Decide what each of you will do.

Act out your play. All your movements should be in slow motion.

Talking It Over

What movements were hardest to make in slow motion? Why do you think so?

Acting with Objects

Warming Up

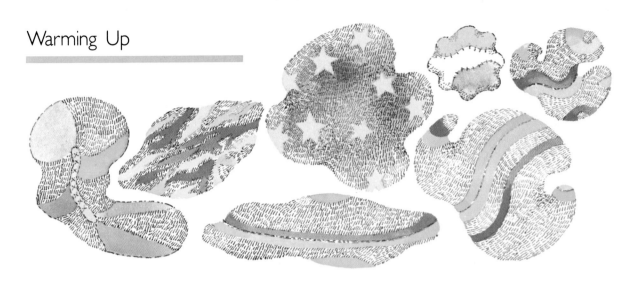

• Imagine you are standing in a circle. You and your friends are throwing a beach ball to one another. This is a special ball. You can change it into any shape.

• You catch the round ball. Use your hands to change its shape. Show, by the way you hold it, the shape of the ball now. Throw the ball to someone.

• The ball is being thrown back to you. It is still the same shape. Show the ball's shape by the way you catch and hold the ball. Use your hands to change the ball's shape. Throw the ball to someone.

• The ball is being thrown back to you. It is a different shape. Show this shape by the way you catch and hold the ball. Use your hands to change the ball's shape. Throw the ball to someone.

Working It Out

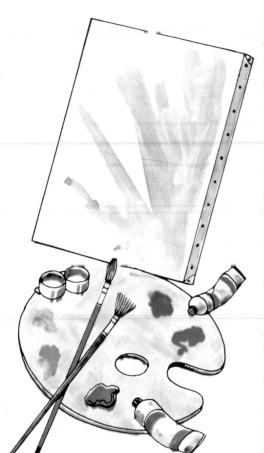

Things, such as the ball, that you use in a play are called **props.** Real props can help you tell stories. Imaginary props can too.

You hold a real glass of water in a certain way. You should hold an imaginary glass of water in the same way. You should remember how big it is. You should remember how heavy it is. You should remember to hold it so as not to spill it.

You drink a real glass of water in a certain way. You should drink an imaginary glass of water in the same way. You should decide how thirsty you are. You should remember how water tastes.

- Imagine you want to make something. Decide what you will make. You may use the things in the picture. You may use anything else.

- Lay out the things you are using in front of you. Begin to work. Use your imaginary tools the way you would use real ones. Remember the size of the thing you are working on.

- When your work is finished, use it. If it is a picture, hang it up. Look at it. If it is something to wear, wear it.

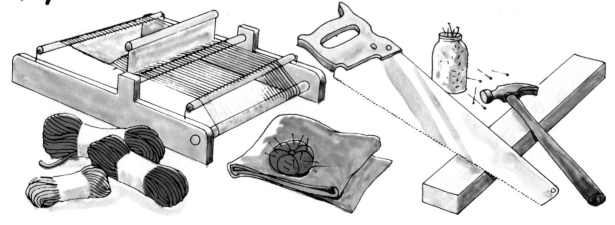

Acting It Out

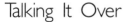

■ Props can be very important in plays. You can make up a play about what happens to a prop. Work with a friend. Choose a prop. It may be one of the things in the picture. It may be something else. One of you has this prop. It is very important to you. Decide why it is important. It might be

—valuable
—filled with information you need
—something you are keeping for someone
—important for another reason

The other of you wants it. Decide why. Decide how you will try to get it. Make up a play about what happens. Decide how your play will end.

Act out your play. Remember to use the prop as if it were real.

Talking It Over

What prop did you use?
How did you show how big it was?
How did you show how heavy it was?
How did you show how important it was to you?

Reviewing Sentence Parts

1. Kinds of Sentences Read each sentence. Write **statement**, **question**, or **command** to show what kind of sentence it is.

If you need help, turn to page 19 of your Practice Handbook.

1. One side is orange.
2. Where shall we meet?
3. Why are you laughing?
4. Come at once.
5. He was not hurt.
6. Wait for us there.
7. The class took a trip.
8. Put your pencils down.
9. Todd fell off his bike.
10. Is Margot ready?

2. The Two Main Parts of a Statement Finish each of these statements. Add a subject to each predicate. Add a predicate to each subject. Write the statements you make.

If you need help, turn to page 20 of your Practice Handbook.

1. |||||||||||||| are huge.
2. |||||||||||||| arrived last night.
3. We |||||||||||||| .
4. Our favorite hiking spot |||||||||||||| .
5. After the hike we |||||||||||||| .
6. Our campsite |||||||||||||| .
7. The horses |||||||||||||| .
8. |||||||||||||| are delicious.
9. |||||||||||||| have been seen.
10. |||||||||||||| seem friendly.

3. Nouns and Determiners in Sentence Subjects Finish each sentence by adding a subject. Your subject should be a **noun** or a **noun with a determiner.**

If you need help, turn to pages 32 and 54 of your Practice Handbook.

1. determiner and noun went by.
2. determiner and noun left early.
3. noun can swim.
4. determiner and noun help Martina.
5. noun taste good.
6. determiner and noun are harmless.
7. noun live in nests.
8. noun are good singers.
9. determiner and noun looked happy.
10. noun gave me a present.

4. Proper Nouns and Pronouns in Sentence Subjects
Finish each sentence by adding a subject. Your subject should be a pronoun or a proper noun.

If you need help,
turn to pages 32 and 55 of your Practice Handbook.

1. ||||||||||| built a boat.
2. ||||||||||| is president of our class.
3. ||||||||||| want to go to the museum.
4. ||||||||||| made a wish.
5. ||||||||||| planned the trip.
6. ||||||||||| wants to be a pilot.
7. ||||||||||| painted a mural.
8. ||||||||||| are very careful.
9. ||||||||||| moved away.
10. ||||||||||| will come tomorrow.
11. ||||||||||| is coming early.
12. ||||||||||| left the house late.

5. Verb Forms The predicates of these sentences are in color. Write the verb from each sentence. Then write **base form, -s form,** or **past tense form** to tell the form of the verb.

If you need help,
turn to pages 36, 37, and 38 of your Practice Handbook.

1. We played a game.
2. After lunch everyone sang a song.
3. Joey plays the piano.
4. Gina and Leo talk to Mr. Alvin.
5. Your sister swims well.
6. A whistle blew.
7. Jenny opened the door.
8. The dog chases the ball.
9. They run every day.
10. The class liked my story.
11. They like to eat carrots.
12. My cat sleeps all day.

6. Nouns as Direct Objects Add a direct object to each sentence. Use a noun alone, a noun with determiner, or a proper noun in each sentence. Write your sentences.

If you need help,
turn to page 43 of your Practice Handbook.

1. Jerry saw   proper noun   .
2. We bought   determiner and noun   .
3. Claudia likes   noun   .
4. The class visited   proper noun   .
5. They picked   determiner and noun   .
6. Celia telephoned   proper noun   .
7. Mr. Sanchez grows   noun   .
8. Look at   determiner and noun   .
9. Miss Jones repairs   noun   .
10. George built   determiner and noun   .
11. They study   determiner and noun   .
12. We like   noun   .

7. Pronouns as Direct Objects Add direct objects to finish these sentences. Use different pronouns. Write the sentences you finish.

If you need help, turn to page 44 of your Practice Handbook.

1. The question surprised ||||||||||||||.
2. Louisa May Alcott wrote ||||||||||||||.
3. Yvonne told ||||||||||||||.
4. Helena will help ||||||||||||||.
5. Ron saw ||||||||||||||.
6. Neville answered ||||||||||||||.
7. The dog chased ||||||||||||||.
8. Patrick drew ||||||||||||||.
9. Their mother called ||||||||||||||.
10. The man stopped ||||||||||||||.

8. Transitive and Intransitive Verbs Find the verb in each sentence. Write **transitive** if the verb is followed by a direct object. Write **intransitive** if the verb is not followed by a direct object.

If you need help, turn to pages 41 and 42 of your Practice Handbook.

1. Mickey asked a question.
2. Gloria answered.
3. We played.
4. Vanessa threw the ball.
5. Philippa caught it.
6. The bears slept.
7. Joel saw a shark.
8. Bells rang.
9. Naomi finished the book.
10. She liked it.

9. Adjectives in Sentence Subjects and Predicates
Write each sentence. Underline the adjective. If the adjective is in the subject, write **subject.** If the adjective is in the predicate, write **predicate.**

If you need help, turn to page 61 of your Practice Handbook.

1. The table was big.
2. Two big chairs were beside it.
3. The peaches were ripe.
4. A ripe banana was in his lunch box.
5. This paint is blue.
6. The blue marker is missing.
7. Many tall trees grow here.
8. Nora is tall.
9. My friends were busy.
10. The busy bees buzzed.

10. Adverbs Find the adverb in each sentence. Write just that word. Then write **where** if the adverb tells where. Write **when** if the adverb tells when. Write **how** if the adverb tells how.

If you need help, turn to page 66 of your Practice Handbook.

1. Breakfast is ready now.
2. Everyone laughed happily.
3. Tina slammed the door loudly.
4. The library is open now.
5. The cat purred softly.
6. We can meet Christa there.
7. Sammy walked slowly.
8. I found your keys upstairs.

11. Yes/No Questions Use the words in each statement to make a yes/no question. Either change the order of the words or add **do**, **does**, or **did**. If you need to, also change the form of one word in the statement.

If you need help, turn to pages 25 and 26 of your Practice Handbook.

1. Your sisters are here.
2. Jocelyn wants to go.
3. They arrive tomorrow.
4. Clara was in a hurry.
5. The rattlesnake was ready to strike.
6. The parks are crowded.
7. Two boxes are missing.
8. Sara looks ill.
9. You could drive the truck.
10. He hit the ball.
11. The sheep need to eat.
12. Those players pitch well.

12. Where-Questions, When-Questions, and How-Questions Read each statement. Write the where-question, the when-question, or the how-question that statement can answer.

If you need help, turn to page 27 of your Practice Handbook.

1. We can swim there.
2. The bus stops here.
3. Sasha waved happily.
4. Otis put the box upstairs.
5. Roses bloom yearly.
6. Traffic is moving slowly.
7. Everyone left quietly.
8. The theater is outdoors.
9. Terence moved cautiously.
10. Jenny is waiting downstairs.
11. The library is closed now.
12. The stranger behaved politely.

13. Who-Questions and What-Questions Read each statement. Write the who-question or the what-question each statement can answer.

If you need help, turn to pages 28 and 29 of your Practice Handbook.

1. Cyrus McCormick invented it.
2. Some games are in it.
3. Lucy ate all of them.
4. Cullen caught them.
5. Josie would like a bicycle for her birthday.
6. A strange noise startled him.
7. Gordon Parks took those pictures.
8. Liz bought some.
9. Teddi found it.
10. Miss Martinez is new this term.

4

Be and Completers

Look at the pictures. How is each thing being completed?

Sentences with **be** also need to be completed. In this chapter, you will learn more about the ways in which such sentences may be completed.

In this chapter, you will learn about

- **be** as a main verb
- nouns as completers
- adjectives as completers
- prepositional phrases as completers

Be as a Main Verb

Read the sentences under the picture.

I **am** surprised now.
Rico **was** surprised yesterday.
Carla **is** surprised now.
His friends **were** surprised yesterday.
My friends **are** surprised now.

• What is the verb in the predicate of each sentence?

   All these verbs are forms of **be.**

• Which forms of **be** are present tense forms?
• Which forms of **be** are past tense forms?

80

Be is a special verb. It has more forms than other verbs. **Am, is,** and **are** are present tense forms of **be.**

- Add a present tense form of **be** to each of these sentences.

1. We ||||||||||||||| speedboat racers.
2. He ||||||||||||||| the captain.
3. They ||||||||||||||| the crew.
4. I ||||||||||||||| the mascot.
5. She ||||||||||||||| the owner of the boat.
6. It ||||||||||||||| a beauty.

Was and **were** are past tense forms of **be.**

- Add a past tense form of **be** to each of these sentences.

1. It ||||||||||||||| a perfect day.
2. The birds ||||||||||||||| in the trees.
3. The sun ||||||||||||||| out.
4. The flowers ||||||||||||||| just about to bloom.
5. The cat ||||||||||||||| on the lawn.
6. We ||||||||||||||| content.

Using What You Have Learned

- Find the form of **be** that is the verb in each of these sentences. Write the verb. Then write **present tense** if it is a present tense form of **be.** Write **past tense** if it is a past tense form of **be.**

1. First I was a carpenter.
2. People were happy with my work.
3. Now I am a contractor.
4. All those houses are mine.
5. You are surprised.
6. It is exciting work.
7. We are interested in science.
8. They were excited.
9. The bank is near.
10. We are students.
11. He was there.
12. The house is too small.

■ ■ Add a form of **be** to each of these sentences. Use present tense forms in sentences 1–10. Use past tense forms in sentences 11–20. Write the whole sentences.

1. She ||||||||||||| the manager.
2. We ||||||||||||| the sales clerks.
3. He ||||||||||||| in charge of complaints.
4. They ||||||||||||| the decorators.
5. I ||||||||||||| interested in getting a promotion.
6. Sam ||||||||||||| in the kitchen.
7. His dogs ||||||||||||| on the porch.
8. Everything ||||||||||||| quiet.
9. We ||||||||||||| surprised by the dogs' barking.
10. It ||||||||||||| time for their supper.
11. The sparrows ||||||||||||| in their nest.
12. She ||||||||||||| interested in watching them.
13. One sparrow ||||||||||||| nervous.
14. Others ||||||||||||| quiet.
15. The cat ||||||||||||| close.
16. The birds ||||||||||||| afraid.
17. The tree ||||||||||||| a safe place.
18. Our dog ||||||||||||| noisy.
19. I ||||||||||||| annoyed by the noise.
20. The neighbors ||||||||||||| too.

Checking Up

Write three sentences. Each sentence should have a different present tense form of **be.** After you have finished, change the verbs in these sentences to the past tense. Write the sentences again.

82

Nouns as Completers

Something To Think About   Read the sentences under the picture.

This is **our team.**
These monsters are **players.**
Our coach is **Mr. W. E. Ird.**

- What is the verb in each sentence?
- In which sentence is the verb followed by a determiner and a noun?
- In which sentence is the verb followed by a noun alone?
- In which sentence is the verb followed by a proper noun?

Nouns can follow the verb **be** in the predicate of a sentence. Nouns can be used as completers.

Sometimes the completer is a noun alone.

Sometimes the completer is a noun with a determiner.

Sometimes the completer is a proper noun. Read the sentences below.

- What is the completer in each sentence?
- Which completers are nouns alone?
- Which completers are nouns with determiners?
- Which completers are proper nouns?

1. They are actors.
2. She is a star.
3. She is Melissa Corbett.
4. Those are books.
5. This is a book.
6. It is *The Return of Dracula*.
7. Here are some records.
8. This is Mr. Chung.
9. That machine is the TV.
10. Those are commercials.

Using What You Have Learned

- Find the noun, the determiner and noun together, or the proper noun after a form of **be** in each of these sentences. Write the completer from each sentence.

1. Those are stores.
2. That is a laundromat.
3. This is Holden's Coffee Shop.
4. This is the turn.
5. That is Sarles Lane.
6. This is home.

■■ Add a noun alone as a completer to each sentence. Then write the sentence.

1. They are ||||||||||||||||.
2. These were ||||||||||||||||.
3. Those are ||||||||||||||||.
4. Here is ||||||||||||||||.
5. This is ||||||||||||||||.
6. We are ||||||||||||||||.

■■■ Add a determiner and noun as a completer to each sentence. Write the sentence.

1. We are ||||||||||||||||.
2. Those were ||||||||||||||||.
3. That was ||||||||||||||||.
4. This is ||||||||||||||||.
5. Here is ||||||||||||||||.
6. They were ||||||||||||||||.

■■■■ Add a proper noun as a completer to each sentence. Write the sentence.

1. We are ||||||||||||||||.
2. The street is ||||||||||||||||.
3. Your school is ||||||||||||||||.
4. We were at ||||||||||||||||.
5. They were ||||||||||||||||.
6. That road is ||||||||||||||||.

Checking Up

Look at the picture at the beginning of the lesson. Write three sentences about it. Use a form of **be** in each sentence. In one sentence use a noun alone as a completer. In another use a noun with determiner as a completer. In another use a proper noun as a completer.

Adjectives as Completers

Something To Think About

Look at the picture of the dodo.

- Add one word to finish each of these sentences about the dodo.

Its wings are very ||||||||||||||||.
Its beak is very ||||||||||||||||.
Its feet are very ||||||||||||||||.
Its tail is very ||||||||||||||||.

Talking Things Over

> It is very ||||||||||||||||.

The words you added, and others like them, are called **adjectives.**

You can use the sentence in the box to test for **adjectives.** Any word that fits in the blank can be an **adjective.**

- Which of these words can be adjectives?

silly	hungry
sad	eat
dinosaur	unusual
useful	television

An adjective often comes after a form of **be** in the predicate of a sentence. Then it is used as a **completer.**

- What adjective is a completer in each of these sentences?

1. Mabel is thirsty.
2. George is hungry.
3. The boys are busy.

4. I am sleepy.
5. Yesterday we were cheerful.
6. It was wonderful.

•• The verb in each sentence is a form of **be.** Add an adjective as a completer to each sentence.

1. Yesterday I was |||||||||||||||.
2. Today I am |||||||||||||||.
3. The monsters were |||||||||||||||.

4. The weather is |||||||||||||||.
5. These fish are |||||||||||||||.
6. You were |||||||||||||||.

Using What You Have Learned

■ Find the adjective that is the completer in each sentence. Write just that word.

1. This TV show is strange.
2. My cat is stubborn.
3. That cake was awful.
4. I am patient.
5. That cabbage is old.
6. Sometimes people are great.

7. The game was long.
8. The end was thrilling.
9. The score was close.
10. Our players were clever.
11. The other team was surprised.
12. The crowd was noisy.
13. Those peanuts are salty.
14. The yarn is tangled.

■ ■ The verb in each of these sentences is a form of **be.** Add an adjective as a completer to each sentence. Write the sentence.

1. Sometimes I am ||||||||||||||.
2. Other times I am ||||||||||||||.
3. Glass slippers are ||||||||||||||.
4. Some games are ||||||||||||||.
5. Applesauce is ||||||||||||||.
6. Superman is ||||||||||||||.
7. Shadows are ||||||||||||||.
8. That beaver is ||||||||||||||.
9. Those planes are ||||||||||||||.
10. Yesterday I was ||||||||||||||.
11. Some stories are ||||||||||||||.
12. This street is ||||||||||||||.
13. The world is ||||||||||||||.
14. Those bees are ||||||||||||||.
15. Today's traffic is ||||||||||||||.

Checking Up

Finish each sentence three times. Use a different adjective completer each time. Write the sentences you make.

Surprises are ||||||||||||||.
That party was ||||||||||||||.

Prepositional Phrases as Completers

Something To Think About

Look at the map of the solar system. Read the sentence beginnings under the map. The first sentence has been finished.

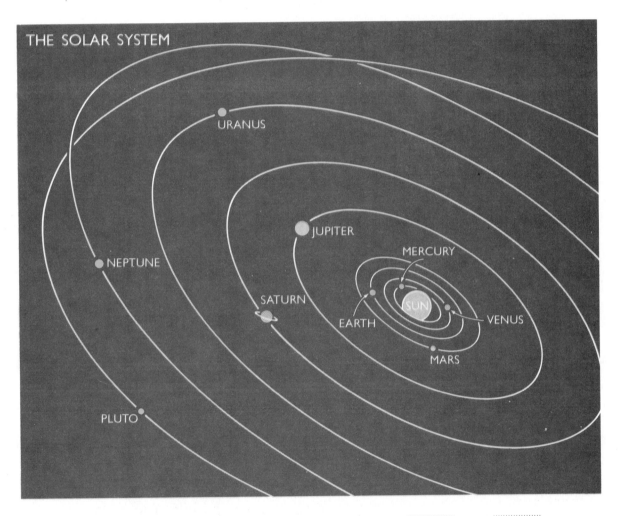

THE SOLAR SYSTEM

URANUS

JUPITER

MERCURY

NEPTUNE

SATURN

SUN

EARTH

VENUS

MARS

PLUTO

The sun is **in** the center .
Mars is **near** ||||||||||||||||.

Mercury is **between** |||||||||||||| and ||||||||||||||.
Many rings are **around** ||||||||||||||.

• Finish the other sentences. Say the sentences you make.

Talking Things Over

with flowers.

toward the monster

to George

about	of
after	off
at	on
before	over
below	through
by	to
during	toward
for	under
from	upon
into	with
near	without

The word in color in each phrase is called a **preposition.** Other prepositions are shown in the blue box.

A preposition can be followed by a noun alone.

A preposition can be followed by a determiner and a noun.

A preposition can be followed by a proper noun.

The preposition and the word or words that follow it are called a **prepositional phrase.**

Prepositional phrases can be completers. A prepositional phrase can follow the verb **be** in the predicate of a sentence.

Read these sentences.

• What prepositional phrase is the completer in each sentence?

1. Mercury is beside the sun.
2. About 50,000 asteroids are in the solar system.
3. Many asteroids are near Mars.
4. Twelve moons are around Jupiter.
5. Mercury, Venus, and Pluto are without moons.
6. Part of Pluto's orbit is inside that orbit.
7. Solid iron is at the center.
8. Molten iron is over that layer.
9. Thick rock is under the crust.
10. We are on the crust.
11. Meteors are in the atmosphere.
12. Water is in this crater.

Read the same sentences again.

- Which prepositional phrase includes a noun alone?
- Which prepositional phrases include a determiner and a noun?
- Which prepositional phrases include a proper noun?

Using What You Have Learned

- Find the prepositional phrase that is the completer in each sentence. Write the prepositional phrase.

1. The people are on horses.
2. The pipe is under the ground.
3. The children are in the car.
4. Balloons are over the city.

5. Everything is in its place.
6. The bird is on the ledge.
7. The streets are near the river.
8. The actors are on the stage.

■■ Add a prepositional phrase as a completer to each sentence. Use a different preposition from the box in each one.

on, in, beside, between, under, behind, over, with

1. The parade is ||||||||||||||.
2. The Queen of the Roses is ||||||||||||||.
3. The clowns are ||||||||||||||.
4. The officials are ||||||||||||||.

Checking Up

Pretend you are on a trip. This trip is to some-place you always wanted to go. Write four sentences telling about it. Use a form of **be** in each sentence. Use a prepositional phrase in each sentence. Each prepositional phrase should come after a form of **be**.

Making Past Tense Verb Forms

| We **look** into the sky now. | We **see** three jets now. |
| We **looked** into the sky yesterday. | We **saw** three jets yesterday. |

Read the sentences in the red box.

- What was added to **look** to make the past tense form?

Read the sentences in the blue box.

- How was **see** changed to make the past tense form?

For Practice

■ The verbs in these sentences change to the past tense form in special ways. Write each sentence. Use the past tense form of the verb in the box.

1. Three girls run in the race.
2. We write letters to our senators.
3. The geese fly south for the winter.
4. The dog bite its trainer.
5. The movie begin at eight o'clock.
6. Our hamsters eat all the carrots.
7. The teacher speak quietly.
8. Terry's parents buy a new apartment.
9. Lucky bring his cousin to the party.
10. Liz and Ray ride their bikes through the park.
11. I sleep until noon last Saturday.
12. The chorus sing three new songs.
13. The farmer sell the fruit at market.
14. She swim to the lighthouse.
15. They break some dishes.
16. He fall down the hill.

Remember

Many verbs add -ed or -d to make the past tense form. But some verbs change in special ways to make the past tense form.

- If you need more help, turn to pages 37 and 38 of your Practice Handbook.

Using Is **or** Are **after** There

There **is** one snake in the big box. There **is** one mouse in the little box.	There **are** two snakes in the big box. There **are** two mice in the little box.

The sentences in both boxes begin with **there.**
Read the sentences in the red box.

- Is each sentence about one thing or more than one thing?
- Which form of **be**—**is** or **are**—is the verb in each sentence?

Read the sentences in the blue box.

- Is each sentence about one thing or more than one thing?
- Which form of **be**—**is** or **are**—is the verb in each sentence?

For Practice

■ Choose **is** or **are** to complete each sentence. Write the sentence.

1. There |||||||||||| seven people in the room.
2. There |||||||||||| some pencils in the cupboard.
3. There |||||||||||| a plant on the windowsill.
4. There |||||||||||| many fish in that river.
5. There |||||||||||| only one cookie left.
6. There |||||||||||| a good show on TV now.
7. There |||||||||||| three robins on the lawn.
8. There |||||||||||| two sails on that boat.
9. There |||||||||||| a cabin near the lake.
10. There |||||||||||| a bug on your arm.
11. There |||||||||||| two cakes in the oven.
12. There |||||||||||| some new books on the shelf.

Remember

Some sentences begin with
There is **or** There are.

Sentences about one person or
thing begin with There is.

Sentences about more than one
person or thing begin with
There are.

◆ If you need more help,
turn to page 48 of your
Practice Handbook.

5
Characters, Settings, and Problems

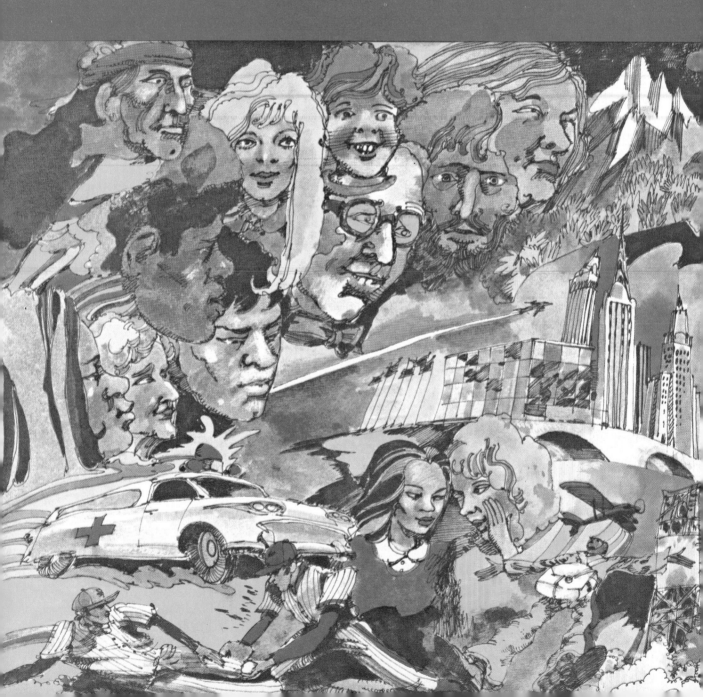

Every story has characters, a setting, and a problem to be solved. The characters are the people or animals in the story. The setting is the place where the story happens. The setting can play a very important part in the story. The characters have a problem. The story tells how they solve their problem.

In this chapter, you will

- make up characters for a story
- describe story settings
- make up and solve a story problem

Writing about Two Story Characters

Looking for Ideas

Look at the characters in the picture. Think about what each character might be like.

Choose one of the human characters.

- List eight words describing what that character might be like.

Choose one of the nonhuman characters.

- List eight words describing what that character might be like.

Talking about Your Ideas

● Pretend you are one of the human characters. Finish these sentences about yourself.

My name is _____.
I live _____.
I am _____ years old.
I spend most of my time _____.
I would like to _____.
I am angry when _____.
I am sometimes afraid of _____.

●● Finish this story about yourself.

Once a very _____ thing happened to me.
I was _____
_____.
I saw _____
_____.
The _____ came toward me.
The _____ wanted _____.
I felt _____. I _____
_____
_____.

●●● Now pretend you are one of the nonhuman characters. Finish these sentences about yourself.

My name is _____.
I am a _____.
I am able to _____.
I spend most of my time _____.
I would like to _____.
I am angry when _____.
I am sometimes afraid of _____.

●●●● Read the story form above again. Use it to tell a story about yourself. Make it different from the story you told before.

Writing about Your Ideas

■ Imagine your two characters are in the same place at the same time. They are on a hill in a very busy city. The street is full of trucks, buses, and cars. The sidewalks are full of people hurrying back and forth.

Suddenly, they hear a voice calling, "Help! Help!"

Decide who is calling for help. Decide why that person needs help. Then think about what each character would do. Decide whether or not the characters will work together.

Write two paragraphs telling what happens. In the first paragraph, tell how the characters react and what they decide to do. In the second paragraph, tell what the characters do.

You may wish to begin your story this way.

Suddenly, a voice called, "Help! Help!" It was ||||||||||||||||||||||||||||||||||||||||||||||||||||||||||||||||||||||||||||||||||||||||||| .

◆ Write another story about your characters. You might want to use one of these ideas:

—the characters go on a trip
—the characters both enter the same contest
—the characters go camping
—the characters go into a haunted house
—the characters go to the circus
—the characters visit a cavern
—the characters go on a rocket

Checking Up

Read your story.

Pick one thing each character did that shows what that character is like. Draw a line under the sentences that tell about it.

Writing about a Story Setting

Looking for Ideas

Look at the pictures of the desert.

- What three words would you use to describe the picture on the left?
- What kind of story might take place in this setting?
- What three words would you use to describe the picture on the right?
- What kind of story might take place in this setting?

Talking about Your Ideas

Many different stories might take place in a desert. In each story, the characters might describe the desert differently.

Imagine you are telling a story about magic in the desert. Two magicians have come to the desert. The magicians need space to work. They don't want anyone to know about their new magic yet. Think of how the magicians would describe the desert at the beginning of the story.

- How would they describe the colors of the desert?
- How would they describe the size of the desert?
- How would they describe the plants and animals in the desert?

Now imagine you are telling a story about creatures from space in the desert. A spacecraft from another world is about to land. This desert is the only part of the planet Earth the creatures in the craft have seen. They think all of Earth is like this desert. Think of how they would describe the desert.

- What might they expect to find in the desert?
- How would they describe the color of the desert?
- How would they describe the size of the desert?
- How would they describe the plants and animals in the desert?
- How would the desert make them feel?

Imagine now that you are telling a story about explorers in the desert. A girl and her brother are exploring the desert alone. They have become lost. They are almost out of water. Think of how they would describe the desert.

- How would they describe the color of the desert?
- How would they describe the size of the desert?
- How would they describe the plants in the desert?
- How would they describe the weather in the desert?

Writing about Your Ideas

- Choose one of the stories that might take place in the desert. Decide how to describe the desert in that story.

Write one paragraph describing the desert. Imagine that this paragraph is the beginning of a story.

- Think about what would happen next in the desert. Write the rest of the story.

Checking Up

Choose one of the other story ideas. Think about how the characters in that story would describe the desert.

Give three ways in which their description would be different from the one in your story.

Writing about a Story Problem

Looking for Ideas

Look at the picture.

- What setting for a story does the picture show?
- What story characters does the picture show?

Talking about Your Ideas

The picture shows a setting and four characters. But the picture does not tell a story.

A story needs a setting and characters. The characters in the story must have a problem to solve. There are different kinds of story problems. Sometimes one character wants something and another wants something else. Sometimes one character wants to do something and another tries to stop him or her. The story shows how the characters try to solve their problem.

You can use the setting and the characters in a story if you add a problem for the characters. Look carefully at the picture of the setting. It might give you an idea of what the characters' problem could be.

- What might the problem be?
- How would the characters solve the problem?
- What would finally happen?

Writing about Your Ideas

■ Use the setting and the characters from the picture in a story. Choose a problem that the characters might have in that setting. Decide how the characters solve their problem. Decide what finally happens.

Write your story.

Checking Up

Read your story.

What things in the setting were part of the characters' problem?

Avoiding Run-On Sentences

Run-on Sentence:	It snowed last night, we can build a snow fort today.
Rewritten Sentences:	It snowed last night. We can build a snow fort today.

Read the sentences in the box.

- How many sentences are in the run-on sentence?
- How was the run-on sentence rewritten?

For Practice

■ Find the nine run-on sentences. Rewrite each run-on sentence as two sentences.

1. The ball was way over Toby's head, he couldn't catch it.
2. We're having a party, I hope you can come.
3. These fresh flowers from the garden smell good.
4. Those flowers are paper, they have no smell.
5. I'm going to the library, I want some new books.
6. That movie was scary, it gave me nightmares.
7. Lucinda and Larry went away to camp last summer.
8. Tracy plays the piano well, she practices every day.
9. The house lights went down, the curtain rose.
10. Our class play was a great success, everyone loved it.
11. Someone has taken the latest copy of my favorite magazine.
12. Let's turn off the TV, I don't like this show.

Remember

Two sentences written as one make a run-on sentence. If you find a run-on sentence in your writing, you should correct it. Rewrite the run-on sentence as two sentences.

♦ If you need more help, turn to page 31 of your Practice Handbook.

Proofreading for Missing Words

> There are many myths and stories $\overset{about}{\wedge}$ about the moon.
>
> Many people think changes in the moon bring good $\overset{or}{\wedge}$ bad luck.

Read the sentences in the box. The writing in red shows how you can add missing words to your writing.

- Where are the missing words written?
- What mark is under each added word?

For Practice

■ Read each sentence. Decide what word is missing. Add that word and write the sentence.

1. Some people wishes on the new moon.
2. Other people believe moonlight can them crazy.
3. The Latin word for moon **luna**.
4. Our word **lunatic** comes **luna**.
5. The moon revolves the earth.
6. The moon's trip around the earth about four weeks.
7. The moon causes ocean tides to move in out.
8. The moon reflects the light the sun.
9. Sometimes the earth comes the moon and the sun.
10. Then people earth see an eclipse of the moon.
11. The is airless, noiseless, and lifeless.
12. Have you ever seen the man the moon?
13. Is moon made of green cheese?
14. Many people thought there canals on the moon.
15. We can only see one side the moon.
16. The moon's surface contains dust rocks.

6
Creating Characters

Look at the pictures. What are the people doing?

In this chapter, you will do many things as you play different characters. You will learn more about how to make your characters seem real.

In this chapter, you will learn how to

- create character objectives
- create characters through dialogue
- show where you are

Creating Character Objectives

Warming Up

Look at each picture.

- Why is each person in the pictures running?
- How do you think each person feels?
- Describe the way each person is running.
- Imagine you are running for fun. You are with a friend. It is a beautiful day. Show how you run.
- It is a very important day at school. You are late. Show how you run.
- It is getting dark. You are hurrying home. Someone is following you. You are afraid. Show how you run.

Working It Out

You had a different reason for running each time you ran. You ran differently each time.

In stories and plays, the characters have reasons for what they do. These reasons are called **objectives.**

This sentence tells about an action.

The girls went to the store.

- What might the girls' objective be?
  Here are two objectives for the girls' action.

  The girls went to the store to buy some milk.
  The girls went to the store to return the things they had stolen.

Read these sentences. Think of an objective for each action.

1. Someone closed the door quickly.
2. Someone tiptoed down the hall.
3. Someone stood looking at the sky.
4. Someone opened the package.
5. Someone slowly counted his money.
6. Someone jumped up and down.

Acting It Out

- You can use one of the actions to make up a story. Work with a friend. Choose an action. Decide who is doing it. Decide what that person's objective is.
  Decide what the other person does.
  Plan how the story begins, what happens next, and how it ends.
  Now act out your story.

Talking It Over

Think about your character's objective. What things did that objective make your character do?

Creating Character Through Dialogue

● Imagine you are a witch or wizard. Use gestures, but no words, to give the message "Come here." Now imagine you are each character below. Use gestures and words to give the same message, "Come here."

—a whining child
—a person who wants his or her own way
—a person who is pleading
—a frightened person
—a worried person
—a happy person
—a mean person
  a sad person
—a crying person

come here
come here
come here come here
come here comehere
come here come here
come here

Working It Out

A person does not always sound the same way.

● Imagine the whining child has been given some candy. The child feels happy and wants to share the candy with a friend. Say "Come here" the way the child would.

● Choose another person you have just acted. That person now feels differently. Decide how that person feels. Say "Come here" the way that person would now.

How a person feels may change the way a person sounds. How a person reacts to someone else may also change how that person sounds.

Look at the pictures.

● Tell what is happening.

Work with a friend. Choose which character in the cartoon you will be. Decide what kind of a person you are. Decide how you feel.

Make up what you and your friend will say.

Act out your story. Use your voice to show who you are. Use your voice to show how you feel.

Acting It Out

Read this story beginning.

Imagine someone decided to throw rocks over a wall to hit some cans.
It was a foolish thing to do. The person throwing the rocks could not see if there was anyone on the other side of the wall. Some small children were playing there. A rock hit one child. The child was badly hurt. The children ran to tell their parents. A parent comes to find the person who threw the rocks.

■ Work with a friend. One of you be the parent. The other be the rock thrower. Decide what kind of person the rock thrower is. The rock thrower might be

—a frightened person
—a bully with a loud voice
—a person like you who knows that he or she has done something foolish
—an angry person
—a person who wants to get away
—a shy person
—any other kind of person

Decide how the parent and the rock thrower will react to each other. Plan how the story will end.
Act out the story.

Talking It Over

What was the rock thrower like?
How did the parent react to this kind of person?

Showing Where You Are

Look at each picture.

- Tell what you see in it.
  Choose one of the pictures. Imagine you work there. Think about what you do there.

- You have just arrived. You get ready for work.

  Choose another picture. Imagine you work there. Look at the things in the picture. Think about how you use them in your work.

- You have just arrived for work. You need to get things ready. Show what you do.

- Now someone has come. Decide why that person has come. Show how you help the person.

Choose another picture. Imagine you work there. Look at the things in the picture. Think about how you use them in your work.

- Show how you get things ready for work.
- Show how you help someone.

Working It Out

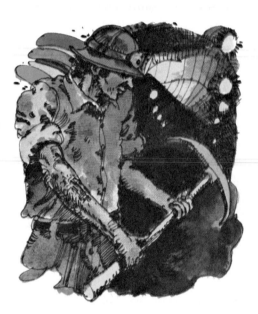

You can show the place where you are by the way you use the things that are there.

Read this list.

a supermarket
a cave
a coal mine
a soda shop
a hospital room
an attic
a laboratory
a dungeon
a team locker room
a cellar
a space station
an amusement park

Choose one place.

- Name five things you would expect to find there.

Picture this place in your mind. Think about where each thing is.

- Imagine you are in this place. Decide how you will use each thing. Show where you are by the way you use each thing. See if others can tell where you are.

Acting It Out

■ Work with a friend. Choose one of the places you talked about. Decide what things are in that place. Picture where each one is.

One of you should be in the place. Decide the kind of person you are. Decide why you are there. Plan what you will do to show this.

One of you comes to the place. Decide what kind of person you are. You have a problem. The problem could be

—something isn't working right
—you don't know what you are supposed to do
—something unexpected has happened
—you are trapped
—anything else

Think about the things that are in the place:

—what things could you use to solve the problem?
—how will you use each one?
—what things might make the problem worse?
—how would each thing make the problem worse?

Plan what each of you will do. Decide how you will act.

Act out your play.

Talking It Over

What things were in the place where you were?

Which ones helped solve the problem?
How did you use each one?

Reviewing the Verb Be and Completers

1. Be as a Main Verb Add a form of **be** to each sentence. Use present tense forms in sentences 1–5. Use past tense forms in sentences 6–10. Write the sentences.

> If you need help, turn to pages 45 and 46 of your Practice Handbook.

1. You ||||||||||| hungry.
2. The cake ||||||||||| stale.
3. I ||||||||||| busy.
4. Our campfire ||||||||||| bright.
5. Those songs ||||||||||| sad.
6. That dinosaur ||||||||||| large.
7. Its legs ||||||||||| thick.
8. One tire ||||||||||| flat.
9. The drawers ||||||||||| empty.
10. I ||||||||||| there.

2. Nouns as Completers Add a completer to finish each sentence. Add just a noun in sentences 1–4. Add a determiner and a noun in sentences 5–8. Use a proper noun in sentences 9–12. Write the sentences you make.

> If you need help, turn to page 47 of your Practice Handbook.

1. Robins are |||||||||||.
2. They are |||||||||||.
3. We are |||||||||||.
4. My brothers are |||||||||||.
5. This room is |||||||||||.
6. Ted is |||||||||||.
7. The sun is |||||||||||.
8. Mars is |||||||||||.
9. Myra's friend is |||||||||||.
10. That boy is |||||||||||.
11. Our class president is |||||||||||.
12. This is |||||||||||.

3. Adjectives as Completers Twelve of these sentences have adjective completers. Write those twelve sentences. Underline the adjective in each sentence.

If you need help, turn to page 65 of your Practice Handbook.

1. My sisters are sad.
2. These packages are light.
3. Mr. Gomez finished the story.
4. The water is cold.
5. The sand is hot.
6. Carla swims.
7. They are tired.
8. Each person is satisfied.
9. The speeches are long.
10. The traffic is heavy.
11. Ms. Long is cheerful.
12. The trip was wonderful.
13. My shoes are tight.
14. The monkeys are playful.
15. Your pen is green.
16. The trip was long.

4. Prepositional Phrases as Completers Add a prepositional phrase as a completer to each sentence. Write the whole sentences.

If you need help, turn to page 70 of your Practice Handbook.

1. The plants were ⦀⦀⦀⦀⦀⦀ .
2. The forks are ⦀⦀⦀⦀⦀⦀ .
3. One monkey was ⦀⦀⦀⦀⦀⦀ .
4. That store is ⦀⦀⦀⦀⦀⦀ .
5. The present was ⦀⦀⦀⦀⦀⦀ .
6. Our street is ⦀⦀⦀⦀⦀⦀ .
7. The boys are ⦀⦀⦀⦀⦀⦀ .
8. My bike is ⦀⦀⦀⦀⦀⦀ .
9. The mailbox was ⦀⦀⦀⦀⦀⦀ .
10. Her skates were ⦀⦀⦀⦀⦀⦀ .
11. Their books are ⦀⦀⦀⦀⦀⦀ .
12. My parents are ⦀⦀⦀⦀⦀⦀ .

7

Words in Subjects and in Predicates

You can be found in many different places. Your friends can be found in many different places. What are some of the places where you can be found?

In this chapter, you will learn more about certain kinds of words and groups of words. You will learn that they can be found in different places in the sentence.

In this chapter, you will learn about

■ nouns in sentence subjects and predicates
■ prepositional phrases in sentence subjects and predicates
■ indefinite pronouns in sentence subjects and predicates

Nouns in Sentence Subjects and Predicates

Two **eagles** soar above us.
Those birds really are **eagles.**
We watch the **eagles.**

Read the sentences under the picture. The word **eagles** is part of all three sentences.

- In which sentences is **eagles** part of the subject?
- In which sentences is **eagles** part of the predicate?
- In which sentence is **eagles** a completer?
- In which sentence is **eagles** part of a direct object?

Eagles is a noun. You can check by putting **eagles** in the test sentence for nouns.

> One eagle is fine,
> but many eagles are better.

Nouns can be in both parts of statements. Nouns can be in the subjects of statements. Nouns can also be in the predicates of statements. Nouns can follow transitive verbs as direct objects. Nouns can also follow forms of **be** as completers.

Each sentence below has only one noun. Find the nouns. Then write your answers to these questions.

- In which sentences is the noun the subject or part of the subject?
- In which sentences is the noun the direct object or part of the direct object?
- In which sentences is the noun the completer or part of the completer?

1. I'll take cake.
2. Roses are red.
3. That is a volcano.
4. They were pilots.
5. Sparrows fly all over.
6. We stewed the meat.
7. The lights were low.
8. She found the nest.
9. The apricots were frozen.
10. We are farmers.
11. She is a lawyer.
12. They broke that dish.

Using What You Have Learned

■ Add the same noun to both sentences in each pair. In the first sentence, the noun will be part of the subject. In the second sentence, the noun will be part of the predicate. Write both sentences in each pair.

1. ||||||||||||| is a metal.
   This ring is |||||||||||||.
2. ||||||||||||| are flowers.
   I planted some |||||||||||||.
3. ||||||||||||| make smoke.
   We built |||||||||||||.
4. ||||||||||||| are animals.
   She likes |||||||||||||.
5. ||||||||||||| crawl along the ground.
   Ms. Chavez studies |||||||||||||.
6. ||||||||||||| is fun.
   Tina and Larry play |||||||||||||.
7. We like to see |||||||||||||.
   ||||||||||||| are entertaining.

8. We ate |||||||||||||.
   ||||||||||||| are delicious.
9. Laura grows |||||||||||||.
   ||||||||||||| are vegetables.
10. Mr. Chin is a |||||||||||||.
    ||||||||||||| do important work.
11. This book is about |||||||||||||.
    ||||||||||||| are interesting to read about.
12. My favorite sport is |||||||||||||.
    ||||||||||||| is exciting.
13. ||||||||||||| come here.
    I can see |||||||||||||.
14. Plants need |||||||||||||.
    ||||||||||||| helps them grow.

■■ Find the noun in each sentence. If it is part of the subject, write **subject.** If it is part of the direct object, write **direct object.** If it is part of the completer, write **completer.**

1. Some dinosaurs were large.
2. Those are their bones.
3. We saw models.
4. That is a brontosaurus.
5. It ate plants.
6. Its tail was long.
7. That is another dinosaur.
8. It ate meat.
9. Another dinosaur could fly.
10. This museum is interesting.

11. It is a new building.
12. Many people worked on it.
13. We can see many things here.
14. Our class wants to come again.

Checking Up

Choose one of these words. Use it in three sentences. In the first sentence, use it as part of the **subject.** In the second, use it as part of the **direct object.** In the third, use it as part of the **completer.**

doctor
clown
firefighter
scientist
dentist
carpenter
astronaut
acrobat

Prepositional Phrases in Sentence Subjects and Predicates

Read the first pair of sentences under the picture. The subject of each sentence is in red.

Felice left the dishes in the sink.
The dishes in the sink are dirty.

Felice put the glasses on the counter.
The glasses on the counter are clean.

- What prepositional phrase is in both sentences?
- In which sentence is the prepositional phrase part of the predicate?
- In which sentence is the prepositional phrase part of the subject?

Read the second two sentences. The subject of each sentence is in red.

- What prepositional phrase is in both sentences?
- In which sentence is the prepositional phrase part of the predicate?
- In which sentence is the prepositional phrase part of the subject?

Talking Things Over

Prepositional phrases can be in both parts of statements. A prepositional phrase can be part of a sentence predicate. A prepositional phrase can also be part of a sentence subject. It may come after the noun in a subject.

Each of these sentences has one prepositional phrase.

- In which sentences is the prepositional phrase part of the predicate?
- In which sentences is the prepositional phrase part of the subject?

1. A worm in the ground is not easily found.
2. A big red balloon has gone to the moon.
3. A pig in a boat will stay afloat.
4. A man from Mars has taken the cars.
5. I'll swallow the pill under the hill.

- Put a prepositional phrase in the blank in each sentence. Say the sentence you make.

1. The hat is ⦚⦚⦚⦚⦚⦚⦚⦚⦚⦚⦚.
2. The clock stopped ⦚⦚⦚⦚⦚⦚⦚⦚⦚⦚⦚.
3. The dancer leaped ⦚⦚⦚⦚⦚⦚⦚⦚⦚⦚⦚.
4. The store ⦚⦚⦚⦚⦚⦚⦚⦚⦚⦚⦚ is expensive.
5. The noise was ⦚⦚⦚⦚⦚⦚⦚⦚⦚⦚⦚.
6. The girl ⦚⦚⦚⦚⦚⦚⦚⦚⦚⦚⦚ spoke softly.

■ Each sentence has one prepositional phrase. Write the prepositional phrase. If the prepositional phrase is in the subject, write **subject.** If it is in the predicate, write **predicate.**

1. The meeting was held before class.
2. The party after school was fun.
3. The people in the submarine were surprised.
4. The creature in front was huge.
5. Another creature lay under the rocks.

■■ Put a prepositional phrase in the blank in each sentence. Write the sentence you make.

1. The noise came ||||||||||||||.
2. The mouse |||||||||||||| squeaked.
3. The cat |||||||||||||| watched.
4. The mouse ran ||||||||||||||.
5. The cat jumped ||||||||||||||.
6. The dog |||||||||||||| growled.
7. The elephants |||||||||||||| were restless.
8. There was a storm ||||||||||||||.
9. Some footprints were ||||||||||||||.
10. The footprints |||||||||||||| had seven toes.
11. These prints went ||||||||||||||.
12. The prints stopped ||||||||||||||.
13. People |||||||||||||| were frightened.
14. Our horses sped ||||||||||||||.
15. It was getting dark ||||||||||||||.
16. Something |||||||||||||| made a noise.

Write a sentence with a prepositional phrase in the subject. Write a sentence with a prepositional phrase in the predicate.

Indefinite Pronouns in Sentence Subjects and Predicates

The sentences under the picture are not complete.

‖‖‖‖‖‖‖‖‖ is on the stairs.
I heard ‖‖‖‖‖‖‖‖‖.
There is ‖‖‖‖‖‖‖‖‖.
‖‖‖‖‖‖‖‖‖ rattled.
‖‖‖‖‖‖‖‖‖ howled.
‖‖‖‖‖‖‖‖‖ came from above.

• Add **some** to each word in the box to make three new words. Use each word in each sentence.

one	thing	body

127

Talking Things Over

The words you made, and others like them, are called **indefinite pronouns.** The words in the box are indefinite pronouns.

- Which indefinite pronoun is written as two words?

anybody	everybody	nobody	somebody
anyone	everyone	no one	someone
anything	everything	nothing	something

An indefinite pronoun may be the subject of a sentence.

- What indefinite pronoun is the subject of each of these sentences?

1. Anyone can do that.
2. Somebody is on the phone.
3. Nothing is the matter.
4. No one went to the beach.
5. Everything is wonderful.
6. Everybody agreed the food was bad.

An indefinite pronoun may also be part of a sentence predicate. An indefinite pronoun may follow a transitive verb as a direct object. An indefinite pronoun may be a completer after a form of **be.**

- What indefinite pronoun is in the predicate of each of these sentences?

1. I didn't see anyone.
2. She saw something move.
3. They took something out of the closet.
4. We knew nobody there.
5. He is somebody famous.
6. Angelica knew no one.

Using What You Have Learned

■ Find the indefinite pronoun in each sentence. Write each indefinite pronoun. Then write **subject** if it is the subject of the sentence. Write **predicate** if it is part of the predicate of the sentence.

1. Somebody will rescue him.
2. She is somebody new.
3. Anyone can do a somersault.
4. No one can jump that high.
5. I can't do anything today.
6. They threw everything out.
7. Nobody is going to the show.
8. I will speak to everyone.
9. We have to do something about it.
10. Anyone can get into the game.

■■ Add a different indefinite pronoun to each sentence. Write the whole sentence.

1. ||||||||||||||| can walk backwards.
2. I can't hear ||||||||||||||| you say.
3. ||||||||||||||| seems to matter.
4. He will be ||||||||||||||| some day.
5. ||||||||||||||| is guilty.
6. They wanted ||||||||||||||| to go away.
7. ||||||||||||||| knows how to fix the car.
8. Perhaps you can get ||||||||||||||| to go with you.
9. ||||||||||||||| is waiting.
10. Clean ||||||||||||||| out of your closet.

Checking Up

Write two sentences with indefinite pronouns as subjects.

Write two sentences with indefinite pronouns as direct objects.

Choosing the Verb Form That Goes with Indefinite Pronouns

> Everyone **sits** quietly.
> Somebody **raises** the curtain.
> Nothing **happens.**

Read the sentences in the box.

- What indefinite pronoun is the subject of each sentence?
- What is the verb in each sentence?
- How does each verb end?

For Practice

■ The subject of each of these sentences is an indefinite pronoun. Choose the verb form that goes with the subject. Then write the sentence.

1. Everyone like, likes ice cream.
2. Somebody slams, slam the door.
3. Nothing bother, bothers Betsy.
4. Everything happens, happen at once.
5. No one leaves, leave the room.
6. Something makes, make a strange noise.
7. Someone know, knows the answer.
8. Everybody go, goes to the park.
9. No one get, gets lost.
10. Everything tastes, taste delicious.
11. Somebody bake, bakes good cookies.
12. Everybody wants, want more cookies.
13. No one come, comes on Tuesday.
14. Anybody work, works better that way.

Remember

Indefinite pronouns such as someone **and** everybody **can be sentence subjects. The present tense verbs that go with these subjects end with** s.

♦ If you need more help, turn to page 59 of your Practice Handbook.

Making Plural Forms

Most Nouns		**Nouns Ending in s, ss, z, sh, ch, tch, and x**	
one table	three tables	a fox	some foxes
this chair	these chairs	one bench	two benches
Nouns Ending in a Consonant and y		**A Few Special Nouns**	
one story	many stories	that child	those children
a penny	some pennies	one tooth	four teeth

Read the singular and plural forms in the box.

- Which nouns are in the singular form?

- Which nouns are in the plural form?

- How is each singular form changed to make a plural form?

For Practice

■ Each of these nouns is in the singular form. Write the plural form of each noun.

1. student
2. dish
3. puppy
4. joke
5. mouse
6. sandwich
7. lady
8. page
9. glass
10. woman
11. bakery
12. picnic

■■ Change the singular noun in each box to the plural form. Write the whole sentence.

1. Three man waited for the bus.
2. Mr. and Mrs. Brown are teacher
3. We went to two party last week.
4. Tess found these box in the attic.

Remember

We add s to most singular form nouns to make the plural forms.

We add es to almost all singular form nouns that end in s, ss, z, sh, ch, tch, or x to make the plural forms.

The singular forms of some nouns end in a consonant and y. To make the plural forms of these nouns, we change the y to i and add es.

We change a few singular nouns, such as child and tooth, in special ways to make the plural forms.

♦ If you need more help, turn to page 33 of your Practice Handbook.

Using Commas

> Our trip began on June 19, 1979.
> We flew to London, England.
> We saw the House of Lords, Buckingham Palace,
>   and the Tower of London.
> Yes, we had a wonderful time.
> Joan, I wish you had been there.

Read the sentences in the box.

- What mark comes between the number of the day and the year in a date?
- What mark comes between the name of a city or town and the name of a country or state?
- What mark comes between names in a series?
- What mark comes after **yes** or **no** at the beginning of a sentence?
- What mark comes after the name of a person being spoken to?

For Practice

■ Write these sentences. Add commas wherever they are needed.

1. Our family had a special party on May 3 1980.
2. Aunt Bobbi came all the way from Tokyo Japan.
3. No Uncle Jason wasn't there.
4. Mom Dad and I cooked all the food.
5. We made chili bread and salad.
6. Craig I wish you could have tasted that chili.
7. Yes it was delicious.
8. We had pie cake and ice cream for dessert.
9. We called Uncle Jason in Waco Texas.

Remember

A comma comes between the number of the day and the year in a date.

A comma comes between the name of a city or town and the name of a state or country.

Three or more names in a row make a series. A comma comes between the names in a series.

A comma comes after yes or no at the beginning of a sentence.

A comma comes after the name of a person being spoken to at the beginning of a sentence.

◆ If you need more help, turn to pages 7, 8 and 10 of your Practice Handbook.

Using Commas with Adjectives

> The **cold, sweet** lemonade tasted good.

Read the sentence in the box.

- What two adjectives come before the noun **lemonade**?
- What mark comes between the two adjectives?

For Practice

■ Find the two adjectives before a noun in each sentence. Write the sentence. Add a comma between the adjectives.

1. We sat under a tall shady tree.
2. The tired hungry hikers finally arrived.
3. Our happy friendly neighbors welcomed us home.
4. Darnell likes hot spicy food.
5. We put the food on small round tables.
6. That warm gentle breeze feels good.
7. The cold deep water looks inviting.
8. That big furry animal is a bear.
9. Everyone sat on the large sturdy bench.
10. Kate opened the small heavy box.
11. The campers sat around a bright hot fire.
12. The sudden loud sound surprised us.
13. Our long red canoe held us all.
14. We rowed down the long winding river.
15. The hungry tired campers arrived.
16. They found a cool dark cave in which to stay.
17. Nearby was a deep blue lake.
18. Everyone swam in the clear cool water.

Remember

Two adjectives, or more, may come before one noun. When they do, a comma usually comes between the adjectives.

- If you need more help, turn to page 12 of your Practice Handbook.

8
Writing for Television

Many people watch television almost every day. Think about the television shows you watch. Think about the shows you like and the shows you do not like. Then suppose you could make up any kind of show you want. What would your show be like?

In this chapter, you will

- plan an evening's television schedule
- create a television series
- write a story for that series
- make up dialogue for your story

Planning a Television Schedule

Looking for Ideas

The boy and girls in the picture want to see something new on TV. They would like to make their own show.

- What kind of show would they like to make?
- What would they call the show?

Talking about Your Ideas

You can make up ideas for television shows. You can plan one evening's schedule of TV shows.

- What different kinds of shows would you make up?

Think about each show you would make up.

- What would it be about?
- What would you call it?
- What time would it be on TV?

Writing about Your Ideas

■ Make up your own television schedule for one day. Think about the different kinds of shows you might make up. Think of what each show should be about. Then make up a name for the show. Decide what time the show should be on.

Write your television schedule. Write the time and the name of each show. Then write one sentence telling what each show is about.

Your television schedule might look like this:

4:30–5:00   **Nature Walk:** Two children examine the life in a local pond.

5:00–5:30   **Book Report:** Actors dramatize a popular children's book.

5:30–6:00   **All-Star Games:** Sportscasters report on the most important sports events of the week.

6:00–6:30   **What Do You Want to Know?** Newscasters report on stories people have asked for.

6:30–7:30   **Our World:** Scientists explain how nature is ruled by laws.

7:30–8:00   **Laugh Class:** A funny teacher helps students learn by telling jokes.

8:00–9:00   **Far Out:** Two teenagers stow away in a rocket headed for Mars.

9:00–10:00   **Creepy Characters:** Monsters from another world take over a school.

Checking Up

How many different kinds of shows are on your schedule?

Creating a Television Series

Looking for Ideas

Read about a new television series.

- What is the name of the series?
- What is the main idea of the series?
- Who are the main characters in the series?
- How does each main character look?
- How do you think each main character acts?

FAR OUT Is a new television series filled with **ADVENTURE AND EXCITEMENT.**

BONITA BRAVO and MELVIN MERCURY

LYDIA LIGHT and DANIEL DANGER

want to travel to new places. They stow away on a rocket bound for Mars. On board they have to face the two astronauts.

It's a long trip to Mars. Each week the stowaways face new dangers. Tune in every Saturday night to see how Bonita and Melvin survive their **FAR OUT** trip.

Talking about Your Ideas

Think about the shows you made up for your television schedule. Imagine you can make one story show into a weekly series.

- Which show would you want to make into a series?
- What would the main idea of the series be?
- Who would be the main characters in the series?
- What would each main character be named?
- How old would each character be?
- How would each character look?
- How would each character act?

Writing about Your Ideas

■ Choose one of the television shows you made up. If you wish, make up another show instead.

Write a plan for that show as a weekly television series. Your plan should be at least three paragraphs.

In the first paragraph tell the name of the series. Also tell the main idea of the series.

In each of the other paragraphs, write about one of the main characters. Tell the character's name and age. Tell how the character looks. Tell how the character acts.

Checking Up

Read the plan you wrote for your television series. Think about your characters. Imagine they are trapped in a room. The only way to get out is to get past a strange, silent animal. They do not know anything about this animal. Tell what each character would do.

Writing a Story for Television

Looking for Ideas

Read this paragraph.

In the television series FAR OUT, Bonita and Melvin have stowed away on a spacecraft bound for Mars. Now they have a problem. They are very, very hungry. They might starve before they get to Mars. Lydia Lite might help them, but they are afraid of what might happen if Daniel Danger finds them. They try to think of a way to talk to Lydia without Daniel hearing. Suddenly Bonita has an idea.

This paragraph tells the beginning of a story but not the end.

- How do you think the story ends?

Talking about Your Ideas

The story you have just made up could be the story of one show in the series FAR OUT.

Think about the television series you made up. Think about what the characters are like and how they act.

Make up a problem for your characters. They might be in a dangerous place.

- Where are they?
- What is the danger?

They might be getting ready for a visitor.

- Who is the visitor?
- What special things must they do to get ready for the visitor? Why must they do them?

They might be going on a trip.

- Where are they going?
- Why must they go there?
- What dangers might occur?

They might be doing anything else.
How will your characters solve the problem?

Writing about Your Ideas

■ You have planned what will happen in your story. Now decide what each character will do. Write your story.

Checking Up

Read your story.

How many characters are in your story?
Choose one of the characters. Draw a line under every sentence that tells about that character.

Writing Dialogue for Your Television Story

Looking for Ideas

The characters in almost all television shows speak. The words they speak are called **dialogue.** Read this dialogue. It is from the television series FAR OUT.

MELVIN: What are we going to do? We're thousands of miles from our own planet. Our food from Earth is long gone. But if Daniel Danger finds out we're on this rocket . . .

BONITA: Don't even mention it! It's too awful to think of what he might do. But we have to get some food somehow. I'm really starving right now.

MELVIN: Do you think Lydia Lite might help us?

BONITA: She seems very kind. She just might want to help us.

MELVIN: Maybe we could talk to her without letting Daniel hear us.

BONITA: That gives me an idea!

This dialogue tells the same story as the paragraph on page 140.

Read that paragraph. Then read the dialogue again.

- What problem does the paragraph say Melvin and Bonita have?
- What lines of dialogue tell about that problem?
- What does the paragraph say about how Bonita and Melvin feel about Daniel Danger?
- What lines of dialogue show the same feeling?

Talking about Your Ideas

• You have already thought of an ending for this story. Now finish the dialogue. Tell what each of the characters says.

Notice how the dialogue for FAR OUT is written. Words such as *said, asked,* and *answered* are not used. Quotation marks are not used either.

• Where is the name of each speaker written?

• What mark comes after the name of each speaker?

Writing about Your Ideas

■ You can turn the story you wrote in the last lesson into a television play. You can do this by writing your story in dialogue.

Read your story carefully. Think about what happens. Think about how each character reacts. Think about what each character would say.

Now write dialogue for your story. Write your dialogue the way the dialogue for FAR OUT is written.

Checking Up

Read your story.

• What were the two most important things that happened?

Read your dialogue.

• Draw a line under the parts of the dialogue that tell about the two most important happenings.

Avoiding Sentence Fragments

Sentence:	Hank slammed the ball over the fence.
Sentence Fragment:	And into the stands.

Rewritten Sentence:	Hank slammed the ball over the fence and into the stands.

Read the groups of words in the first box.

- Which word group is a sentence?
- Which word group looks like, but is not, a sentence? What is it called?

Read the sentence in the second box.

- How was the sentence fragment rewritten?

For Practice

■ Read each pair of word groups. Find the six pairs that include sentence fragments. Rewrite each sentence fragment as part of the sentence with it.

1. Yvonne ran down the stairs. And out the door.
2. I can meet you here. Or at the bus stop.
3. Nearly all plants make their own food. Animals cannot make food.
4. Animals must eat plants. Or other animals.
5. Our tennis class meets every Tuesday. At four o'clock.
6. The moon has no wind. And no weather.
7. The little dog chased the big cat. Up the tree.
8. The telephone rang. Everyone jumped up.

Remember

A word group that looks like, but is not, a sentence is a sentence fragment. If you find a sentence fragment in your writing, you should correct it. Usually you can rewrite a sentence fragment as part of a whole sentence.

- If you need more help, turn to page 30 of your Practice Handbook.

Writing Direct Quotations

> *"Born Free* is about Elsa," said Amy.
> "Isn't Elsa a lioness?" asked Josh.

> *"Born Free,"* said Amy, "is about Elsa."
> "Isn't Elsa," asked Josh, "a lioness?"

Read the sentences in the boxes. Each sentence has a direct quotation.

- What is the direct quotation in each sentence?
- What marks are in each quotation? Where are they?
- Where are the capital letters?

For Practice

■ Write these sentences. Add capital letters, quotation marks, commas, and question marks wherever they are needed.

1. Joy Adamson found Elsa in Africa said Ray.
2. Bea asked how old was Elsa then?
3. Elsa was just a cub explained Lina.
4. Elsa and her two sisters said Jon were only a few days old.
5. Tanya said the cubs' mother had been killed.
6. Joy Adamson said Marty fed the cubs milk.
7. The lion cubs grew quickly said Ian.
8. What happened asked Dora to Elsa's sisters?
9. Bonita explained they went to a zoo in Holland.
10. What finally happened to Elsa asked Brad.

Remember

A direct quotation tells the exact words a person says. Each direct quotation begins and ends with quotation marks.

Each quotation begins with a capital letter.

When the words that tell who is speaking come after the quotation, a comma or a question mark comes before the end quotation mark.

When the words that tell who is speaking come before the quotation, a period or a question mark comes before the end quotation mark.

In some sentences, the words that tell who is speaking come in the middle of the direct quotation. Quotation marks come at the beginning and the end of each part of the direct quotation. A comma comes after the words in the first part of the direct quotation. Another comma comes after the words that tell who is speaking.

◆ If you need more help, turn to pages 15 and 16 of your Practice Handbook.

Changing Indirect Quotations to Direct Quotations

> Renee said that the guitar is easy to play.
> Renee said, "The guitar is easy to play."
>
> Daryl said that he wants to take guitar lessons.
> Daryl said, "I want to take guitar lessons."

Read the sentences in the box. The first sentence in each pair includes an indirect quotation.

- Which two sentences include direct quotations?
- What word is in both the sentences with indirect quotations, but not in the sentences with direct quotations?

- What punctuation marks are only in the sentences with direct quotations?
- Which words in the second direct quotation are different from the second indirect quotation?

For Practice

■ Rewrite each sentence. Change the indirect quotation to a direct quotation.

1. Quentin said that most guitars have six strings.
2. Belle said that some guitars have twelve strings.
3. Rita said that banjos are similar to guitars.
4. Corene said that a banjo usually has five strings.
5. Randy said that his mother plays the banjo.
6. Lisa said that she likes ukuleles better than guitars.
7. Luz said that she can play seven different chords on a ukulele.
8. Mr. Rochelle said that there are many other stringed instruments.
9. Lorin said that violins have strings.
10. Jeff said that mandolins and zithers have strings too.

- If you need more help, turn to pages 15 and 16 of your Practice Handbook.

Proofreading for Spelling Mistakes

> ~~desserts~~ deserts
> Are all ~~desserts~~ sandy?
> Some deserts ~~our~~ are covered with rocks.

Read the sentences in the box. Notice the red writing.

- How can you correct a misspelled word in your writing?

For Practice

■ Find the misspelled word in each sentence. Correct the spelling of that word. Then write the sentence.

1. Oher deserts are mountainous.
2. Some deserts are even covered wit salt.
3. All deserts have extreme clinates.
4. The temperature changes from very hat to very cold in one day.
5. The Sahara Desert may be as hot as 126° dring the day.
6. At nite the temperature in the Sahara may be only 26°.
7. There is very little watar in a desert.
8. Soemtimes there is no rain for two or three years.
9. When it does rane, there may be a flash flood in the desert.
10. The wind in a desert is usually quiet strong.
11. A large desert stretches threw the western United States and Mexico.
12. The Sahara in northern Africa covers abut three million square miles.

Writing Plays

I only have the title of the play.

I have only the ending of a story.

How can I make up a play from just that?

There are many ways to start to make up a play. In this chapter, you will learn some of them.

In this chapter, you will learn how to

- make entrances and exits
- make up a play from a title
- make up a play from an ending

Entrances and Exits

- Imagine you are very cold. Every part of your body is cold. You have no gloves on. Your hands are almost frozen. Show how you try to keep them warm.

- Your shoes are thin. It is painful to walk. Show how you walk.

- The street goes up a slippery hill. Show how you walk.

- You find a package. It is tied with a string. Your fingers are sore and stiff. Show how you open the package.

- There are mittens in the package! Show how you put them on.

- Finally you enter a warm room. Show how you act.

Working It Out

When an actor or an actress comes on stage, it is called an **entrance.**

When an actor or an actress leaves the stage, it is called an **exit.**

The way you enter shows many things. It can show where you came from. It can show how you feel. What you do just after you enter also shows these things.

The way you exit shows many things. It can show where you are going. It can show how you feel. What you do just before you leave also shows these things.

Look at this picture.

- Describe this setting.

  You might enter it in different ways.

- You have walked home from school in a heavy rain. Show how you enter. Show what you do next.

- You have been chased by someone you are afraid of. Show how you enter. Show what you do next.

- This is a day when everything seems to have gone wrong. Show how you enter. Show what you do next.

  You might leave the room in different ways.

- You have to go out into a bad storm. You don't want to go. Show how you get ready for the storm. Show how you leave.

- You are going to play softball. This is the first time you will pitch. You are very excited. Show how you get ready. Show how you leave.

- You did not finish your homework yesterday. In a few minutes you must leave for school. Show what you do. Show how you leave.

Acting It Out

- Make up a play that has an entrance and an exit.

You will enter through the door on the left. Answer these questions about your entrance.

—From where are you coming?
—What happened to you there?
—How do you feel about it?

Plan how you will show these things.
You will find the note on the table. The note will tell you to go somewhere. Answer these questions about your exit.

—Where are you going?
—How do you feel about it?
—What must you do before you go?

Act out your play.

Talking It Over

How did you show where you had been?
How did you show the way you felt about it?
How did you show where you were going?
How did you show the way you felt about it?

Starting with a Title

Look at the picture. Name the places in it.

- Choose one of the places. Imagine you are there. Think how you would move around there. Explore the place. Touch what it is safe to touch. Make sure you don't touch anything else.

- You are still in the same place. You are looking for something. Decide what you are looking for. Show how you look for it.

Working It Out

Read these titles.

Pick one title. Think what a play with that title might be about.

THE MISSING TOWN

Dora Captures an Elephant

The Marooned Spacecraft

A STRANGE TRIP

Lost in the Underground City

THE HARDEST CLIMB

The Magic Piano

City Under Water

LAST MINUTE SCORE

The Ghost Ship

- Where might the story take place? Describe this place.
- Who are the characters? What are their objectives?
- What problem do the characters have?
- How do they solve the problem?

Acting It Out

■ Work with friends. Choose one of the titles you talked about. Make up a play about it.

First answer the same questions you did before.

Then decide who will play each part. Plan what you will say and do.

Now act out your play.

Talking It Over

Think about your play.

Which part did you like least? How could you improve it?

Starting with an Ending

Warming Up

It is the end of the day.

• You have been working in your garden. You enjoy it, but you are getting tired. You are pulling out the weeds from among the flowers. You work slowly and carefully. Show how you do it.

You want to plant some tomato plants. You bring over the plants. You dig some holes. You plant the plants. Then you put dirt around them and water them. You are becoming more stiff and tired.

• You are six years old. You are playing ball outside after dinner. You are a little tired but you do not want to stop. You are having too good a time. Show how you play.

Your mother calls you to come in. Show how you react.

You don't want to stop. You decide you have to. Show how you walk back to the house.

Working It Out

You have acted out the endings of two stories. You can start with an ending and make up a play.

Read these endings. Answer the questions.

Angrily, the person walked out of the room. The door slammed loudly.

- Who is the person?
- What has made the person angry?
- Why did the person think leaving was the only thing to do?

The plan had worked. The river had overflowed. The town was flooded, but everyone was safe.

- What was the plan?
- Who had made it work? What had these people done?
- What dangers had there been in carrying out the plan?

There they were, only a few yards from their ship. They had gotten what they had come for. As soon as they crossed those few yards, they would be safe.

- Who are "they"?
- Where are they?
- What did they come to get?
- Why do they want it?

At last, they escaped safely to the car. They saw the burning tower in the background.

- Who are "they"?
- Where did they escape from?
- How did the tower catch fire?

Acting It Out

■ Work with friends. Choose one of the endings. Make up a play that leads up to that ending. If you wish, use an ending you have made up.

Think about what led up to that ending. These questions may help you.

—Who are the characters?
—What is each character's objective?
—What problem do the characters have?
—How do they solve their problem?

Make up your play. Then decide who will play each part. Plan what you will do and say.

Act out your play.

Talking It Over

Who were the characters in your play?

What did each character do that helped lead to the ending?

Reviewing Words in Subjects and in Predicates

1. Nouns in Sentence Subjects and Predicates
Write each sentence. Underline the noun. If the noun is in the subject, write **subject**. If the noun is in the predicate, write **predicate**.

If you need help,
turn to pages 32 and 43 of
your Practice Handbook.

1. One book is left.
2. He needs that book.
3. Some birds sing loudly.
4. We studied the stars.
5. We heard a sound.
6. It was the telephone.
7. The bottle was empty.
8. She found the paints.
9. The door is open.
10. She opened the door.
11. The broom was here.
12. They have caught the fish.

2. Prepositional Phrases in Sentence Subjects and Predicates Write each sentence. Underline the prepositional phrase. If the prepositional phrase is in the subject, write **subject**. If the prepositional phrase is in the predicate, write **predicate**.

If you need help,
turn to pages 71 and 72 of
your Practice Handbook.

1. Doug waited behind the door.
2. The electricity in this neighborhood is off.
3. My sisters are in the park.
4. The boy with them is my cousin.
5. Craig's grandmother is in Indiana.
6. The name of this parakeet is Perry.
7. The animals at the zoo are wild.
8. The animals are in cages.
9. The day before yesterday was Tuesday.
10. My birthday is in March.

Add a prepositional phrase to each sentence.
Write the sentence.

1. The girl ||||||||||||||| is Ruth.
2. The people ||||||||||||||| are tired.
3. Put the apples |||||||||||||||.
4. The nest ||||||||||||||| is full of robins.
5. A cat ||||||||||||||| is sneaking up.
6. One robin ||||||||||||||| sees the cat.
7. The robins fly |||||||||||||||.
8. The cat goes |||||||||||||||.
9. The pictures ||||||||||||||| are old.
10. My watch is |||||||||||||||.

3. Indefinite Pronouns Add an indefinite pronoun
to each sentence.

1. We saw |||||||||||||||.
2. ||||||||||||||| saw us.
3. ||||||||||||||| pounded on the door.
4. The bus driver forgot |||||||||||||||.
5. ||||||||||||||| hurried past us.
6. She helps |||||||||||||||.
7. ||||||||||||||| closed the windows.
8. This glue holds |||||||||||||||.
9. ||||||||||||||| could have done that.
10. ||||||||||||||| knew the answer.

If you need help,
turn to pages 59 and 60 of
your Practice Handbook.

Find the indefinite pronoun in each sentence.
Write only the indefinite pronoun. Then write
subject if it is in the subject. Write **predicate**
if it is in the predicate.

1. Someone saw him.
2. Everybody helped.
3. No one answered.
4. Did you see anyone?
5. She spoke to everyone.
6. Something moved.
7. They asked nobody.

10
Verb Forms
That End in -ing and -n

Look at the pictures. In which pictures are people doing something? In which pictures have they finished doing it?

In this chapter, you will learn about two verb forms. You will also learn about some of the ways we show **when** something happens.

In this chapter, you will learn how to

- recognize **-ing** form verbs with **be**
- use **-ing** form verbs with **be**
- recognize **-n** form verbs with **have** and **has**
- use **-n** form verbs with **have** and **has**
- recognize other **-n** form verbs with **have** and **has**
- use other **-n** form verbs with **have** and **has**
- show when something happens

Recognizing -ing Form Verbs with Be

Something To Think About

These people **enjoy** the roller coaster.
The people **are enjoying** the roller coaster.

Read the sentences above the picture. The verb in each sentence is in blue.

- Are the sentences about **now** or **yesterday?**
- How are the verbs different?
- What word is only in the predicate of the second sentence?

Talking Things Over

The verb **enjoy** is in both sentences. Look at the verb in the first sentence.

- What form of the verb is in this sentence? How do you know?

162

Look at the form of **enjoy** in the second sentence.

• How is it different? This form of the verb **enjoy** is called the **-ing** form.

• What word goes with **enjoying** in the second sentence?

Now read the sentences in the boxes.

> These people **are enjoying** the roller coaster.

> She **is enjoying** the roller coaster.

• What word goes with **enjoying** in the sentence in the red box?
• What word goes with **enjoying** in the sentence in the blue box?

Is, am, and **are** can go with **enjoying.**

• Find the sentences that have a form of **be** before the verb. Read these sentences. Say the form of **be** and the **-ing** verb form.

1. I am driving past the airport.
2. A crowd is looking into the sky.
3. People are pointing at something.
4. A strange craft is approaching.
5. It is landing at the airport.
6. The craft comes to a stop.
7. A wailing sound comes from the craft.
8. Nobody in the crowd is making a sound.
9. All the people are watching the craft.
10. Slowly, three doors are opening.

■ Find the sentences that have a form of **be** in them. Write only those sentences. Draw a line under the form of **be** and the **-ing** verb form.

1. A guard is moving toward the craft.
2. He is walking right into the craft.
3. A very loud sound comes from inside.
4. People are running away.
5. One other person is going toward the craft.
6. She climbs on top of the craft.
7. I am sneaking toward it too.
8. The woman is creeping toward the door.
9. Suddenly something pulls her inside.
10. I am coming closer to the third door.
11. I try to peek in.
12. Something is pulling me inside.
13. I am struggling.
14. The thing is holding me.
15. Something is pulling the woman inside too.
16. I am holding the door.
17. The thing pulls me inside.
18. I am looking around.

■ ■ Write two sentences about what happens inside the craft. Use a form of **be** and the **-ing** verb form in each sentence.

Checking Up

Read the verb forms in the box. Write only the **-ing** forms.

riding	learning	think	explain
talk	reading	hiding	singing
flying	sing	hope	preparing
happening	working	saying	rush

Using -ing Verb Forms with Be

Something To Think About

The race **starts.**
The race **is** |||||||||||||||| .

The skaters **go** around the curve.
The skaters **are** |||||||||||||||| around the curve.

Read the sentence under the first picture.

• Which word in the sentence is the verb?
• Use a form of that verb to finish the second sentence. Say the whole sentence.
• How did you change **starts** to use it in the second sentence?

Read the sentence under the second picture.

• What word in the sentence is the verb?
• Use a form of the verb to finish the second sentence. Say the whole sentence.
• How did you change **go** to use it in the second sentence?

The verb **start** is in both sentences under the first picture.

- What form of **start** is in the first sentence?

The **-ing** form of **start** is in the second sentence.

- What word comes before **starting** in the second sentence?

The verb **go** is in both sentences under the second picture.

- What form of **go** is in the first sentence?
- What form of **go** is in the second sentence?
- What word comes before **going** in the second sentence?

A form of **be** comes before the **-ing** form of the verb.

- Read these sentences. Find the form of **be** and the **-ing** verb in each one.

1. She is falling.
2. Benny was laughing.
3. Two small boys were running.
4. Five big dogs are barking.
5. I am talking.
6. Lisa is listening.
7. They are writing.
8. Cara and Kenneth were cooking.
9. The car was turning.
10. Inez and Ben are racing.
11. Vacation is coming.
12. The weather is changing.
13. Keith is swimming in the pond.
14. The speedboat is cutting through the water.
15. Our cat was scratching at the door.

● Finish each sentence in two ways. First write the sentence using the **-s** form of the verb. Then write the sentence using **is** and the **-ing** form.

1. Marva |||||||||||||||| a sweater. (knit)
2. Roxanne |||||||||||||||| everywhere. (look)
3. Our sand castle |||||||||||||||. (collapse)
4. The baby |||||||||||||||. (laugh)

Using What You Have Learned

■ Find the verb in the first sentence of each pair. Use the **-ing** form of that verb to finish the second sentence. Write the sentence.

1. Dolores walks up the stairs.
   Dolores is |||||||||||||||| up the stairs.
2. The stairs creak.
   The stairs are ||||||||||||||||.
3. The wind moans.
   The wind is ||||||||||||||||.
4. The lights go out.
   The lights are |||||||||||||||| out.
5. A window pane breaks.
   A window pane is ||||||||||||||||.
6. The front door flies open.
   The front door is |||||||||||||||| open.
7. Lightning strikes a tree outside.
   Lightning is |||||||||||||||| a tree outside.
8. Rain pours in from the door and window.
   Rain is |||||||||||||||| in from the door and window.
9. A bat screeches in the dark.
   A bat is |||||||||||||||| in the dark.
10. Something crashes down the stairs.
    Something is |||||||||||||||| down the stairs.

■■ Add one more sentence to the story. Tell what is crashing down the stairs. Use a form of **be** and the **-ing** form of the verb.

■■■ Finish each sentence two ways. First write the sentence using the **-s** form of the verb. Then write it using the **-ing** form. Remember to use a form of **be** before the **-ing** form.

1. Charlie |||||||||||||| the floor. (sweep)
2. Karl |||||||||||||| to the game. (go)
3. Paula |||||||||||||| tennis. (play)
4. She |||||||||||||| Carole there. (meet)
5. Sammy |||||||||||||| slowly. (walk)
6. He |||||||||||||| the note silently. (read)
7. Jim |||||||||||||| worried. (look)
8. I |||||||||||||| carefully. (watch)
9. Nell |||||||||||||| Ted. (call)
10. Ms. Nakamara |||||||||||||| here. (work)

■■■■ Add **be** and an **-ing** form verb to each sentence. Write the sentence.

1. The clown |||||||||||||| in the ring. (dance)
2. Acrobats |||||||||||||| on the trampoline. (bounce)
3. Tigers |||||||||||||| in their cage. (roar)
4. Elephants |||||||||||||| for the audience. (perform)
5. Two men |||||||||||||| the horses. (ride)
6. Vendors |||||||||||||| hot dogs. (sell)
7. People |||||||||||||| spun candy. (buy)
8. We |||||||||||||| high in the balcony. (sit)
9. The seals |||||||||||||| their fins. (clap)
10. The children |||||||||||||| at the clowns. (laugh)

Checking Up

Write each sentence three times. Use a different verb each time.

Frank is |||||||||||||| today.
Delia is |||||||||||||| now.

Recognizing -n Form Verbs with Have and Has

Read the sentences under the picture. The verb in each sentence is in blue.

They **took** the meat.
They **have taken** the meat.

- How are the verbs different?
- What word is in the predicate of only the second sentence?

The verb **take** is in both sentences.

- What form of **take** is in the first sentence?
- What form of **take** is in the second sentence?
- What word goes with **taken** in the second sentence?

This form of the verb **take** is called the **-n** form.

Now read the sentence in the box.

> The big dog has taken some meat.

- What word goes with **taken** in this sentence?

  Have and **has** can go with **taken**. These words are forms of **have**.

- Find the **-n** form verbs after **have** and **has** in these sentences.

1. Carla has driven there before.
2. They have eaten.
3. Her aunt has given her a present.
4. We haven't seen him.
5. The cat has broken the vase.
6. The ponds have frozen.
7. The team has chosen a captain.
8. The birds have flown away.
9. How you have grown!
10. Ms. Wong has written a book.
11. The dam has broken!
12. They have beaten the record.

Using What You Have Learned

- Find the sentences with **have** or **has** and an **-n** form verb. Write only those sentences.

1. He has spoken to them before.
2. The dog has stolen a bone.
3. The wind has blown all day.
4. It blew the tree down.
5. Jill has known for a week.
6. The sails have torn.
7. They saw it yesterday.
8. We hid the presents.
9. We have hidden them in the attic.
10. Jerry flew over the city.
11. Margaret has flown over it many times.
12. The leaves have fallen.

Checking Up

Read the verb forms in the box. Write only the **-n** forms.

chose	knew	rode	blown
wrote	grown	choose	ridden
written	driven	taken	known
shaken	stolen	eaten	fallen

Using -n Form Verbs with Have and Has

Something To Think About

The dinosaur **fell.**
The dinosaur has ||||||||||||||||

People **saw** the bones.
People have |||||||||||||||| the bones.

Read the first sentence in each group.

• Which word in each sentence is the verb?
• What form of the verb is it?
• Use a form of that verb to finish the second sentence. Say the whole sentence.
• What form of each verb did you use to finish the sentence?

Talking Things Over

● Read these verbs. Change them to the **-n** form. Say each **-n** form verb with **have.**

shake	bite	write	ride
grow	break	drive	eat
choose	see	throw	wore
give	blow	freeze	fly

● Use the **-n** form verb to finish each sentence.

1. The mosquitos have ||||||||||||||| John badly. (bite)
2. Sal has ||||||||||||||| that horse. (ride)
3. The news has ||||||||||||||| the whole town. (shake)
4. I have ||||||||||||||| the record. (break)
5. Janice has |||||||||||||||. (fly)
6. Norman has ||||||||||||||| the secret. (know)
7. They have ||||||||||||||| a house. (see)
8. The outfielder has ||||||||||||||| the ball! (throw)
9. The wind has ||||||||||||||| away the fog. (blow)
10. Our coach has ||||||||||||||| a holiday. (take)

Using What You Have Learned

■ Find the verb in the first sentence of each pair. Use another form of that verb to finish the second sentence. Write the sentences you finish.

1. Maria drew a picture.
   She has ||||||||||||||| many pictures.
2. Let's take the road through the mountains.
   I have ||||||||||||||| that road many times.
3. Louis drove Miss Chang's car.
   He has ||||||||||||||| it before.
4. Our class saw the movie.
   We have ||||||||||||||| it before.

5. The lake froze.
   It has ⦀⦀⦀⦀⦀⦀ every winter.
6. I ate a sandwich.
   Beverly has ⦀⦀⦀⦀⦀⦀ one already.
7. Pat grew these roses.
   He has ⦀⦀⦀⦀⦀⦀ roses for three years.
8. The puppy bit me.
   It has ⦀⦀⦀⦀⦀⦀ me before.
9. Blake tore the newspaper.
   He has ⦀⦀⦀⦀⦀⦀ it.
10. Luis fell off the stage.
    He has ⦀⦀⦀⦀⦀⦀ off it before.
11. Our club gave a Halloween party.
    We have ⦀⦀⦀⦀⦀⦀ one every year.
12. Terese rode a unicycle.
    She has ⦀⦀⦀⦀⦀⦀ one before.
13. We chose the first answer.
    We have ⦀⦀⦀⦀⦀⦀ the wrong one.
14. The man wove the rug.
    The man has ⦀⦀⦀⦀⦀⦀ the rug.

Checking Up

Finish each sentence two ways. First write the sentence using the **past** form of the verb. Then write the sentence using **have** or **has** with the **-n** form of the verb.

1. Kim ⦀⦀⦀⦀⦀⦀ the prizes. (hide)
2. The scouts ⦀⦀⦀⦀⦀⦀ the mountain. (see)
3. The strange beings ⦀⦀⦀⦀⦀⦀ old machines. (drive)
4. Claudia ⦀⦀⦀⦀⦀⦀ quietly. (speak)
5. The cat ⦀⦀⦀⦀⦀⦀ the food. (eat)
6. The vase ⦀⦀⦀⦀⦀⦀ in the fall. (break)
7. We ⦀⦀⦀⦀⦀⦀ to her often. (speak)

Other -n Form Verbs

The cat **broke** the vase.
The cat has |||||||||||||| the vase.

Read the first sentence under the picture.

- What is the verb in the sentence?

Finish the second sentence. Use a form of the verb in the first sentence.

- What form of the verb did you use?
- What word goes with **broken**?

Read the sentences under the pictures.

They **made** popcorn.
They have **made** popcorn.

The cat **crept.**
The cat has **crept** to the bowl.

The cat **finished** the popcorn.
The cat has **finished** the popcorn.

Answer these questions for each pair of sentences.

- What is the verb in the first sentence?
- What is the verb in the second sentence?
- What word comes before the verb in the second sentence?

Talking Things Over

In the second sentence of each pair, the verb comes after **have** or **has.** Any verb that comes after **have** or **has** is called an **-n** form verb. An **-n** form verb does not have to end with **n.** It can end with many different letters.

- Find the **-n** form verbs after **has** or **have** in each sentence.

1. His friend has lent him the money.
2. Many ships have sunk near there.
3. Paul has said that many times.
4. The kittens have drunk all the milk.
5. We have caught many fish.
6. The dam has burst!
7. A bee has stung me!
8. Nora has laid the books on the table.
9. The sun has risen.
10. The chorus has sung already.
11. The animals have crept closer.
12. Ms. Browning has led many hikes.

■ Find the sentences with **-n** form verbs. Write
only those sentences.

1. Jeremy has lost his watch again.
2. I saw it on the table.
3. Phillip and Rozalind have seen it too.
4. Class has begun.
5. Please begin your work.
6. Who has brought lunch?
7. They have come late.
8. Marc has set the table.
9. Laura has walked the whole way.
10. The play has ended by now.
11. Mr. Nakamura has explained the problem.
12. The girls have listened carefully.
13. Together they have solved it.
14. Everyone has helped.
15. They have made everything work.
16. She has sung.
17. The class has gone there.
18. We went last year.
19. People have left.
20. Toby has ridden there before.
21. He rode over that trail.
22. The town has changed.
23. Who has finished?
24. They have finished.

Finish each sentence three times. Each time
use a different **-n** form verb.

1. Barbara has ||||||||||||||||.
2. We have ||||||||||||||||.
3. Jack and Sylvia have ||||||||||||||||.

Showing When Something Happens

I work every day.
I teach these boys and girls every Wednesday.
I am teaching them now.

Read the sentences under the picture.

● Which sentence tells about something that happens every day?
● What form of the verb is used in this sentence?
● Which sentence tells about something that happens every Wednesday?
● What form of the verb is used in this sentence?
● Which sentence tells about something that is happening now?
● What form of the verb is used in this sentence?

Talking Things Over

You can show when something is happening. You can show if something is happening now. You can show if something happens more than once.

Read the sentences under the picture again.

● Which two sentences tell about something that happens more than once?

● Read each sentence. If the sentence tells about something that is happening now, say **now.** If the sentence tells about something that happens more than once, say **more than once.**

1. Dolores trains the elephants every morning.
2. Martin is feeding the lions now.
3. The tigers walk into the ring every day.
4. The trainer is watching one tiger.
5. The show goes on every day.
6. Wolfgang leads the band for every show.
7. Sausita is riding bareback.
8. Beatrice prints new programs every Monday.
9. The parade is going by now.
10. The whole circus parades every day.

Using What You Have Learned

■ Read each sentence. If the sentence tells about something that is happening now, write **now.** If the sentence tells about something that happens more than once, write **more than once.**

1. The library is open each night.
2. We go on Tuesdays.
3. I am reading the sign.
4. There is a game every Friday.
5. Our team is winning.
6. We are all cheering now.
7. Norma is taking a picture.
8. She attends every game.
9. The train is coming.
10. People are waiting.

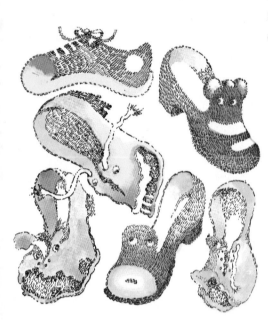

■■ Finish each sentence. If the box at the end says **now,** add **now.** If the box says **more than once,** add words that tell when.

1. We are going now .
2. Mara goes to school more than once .
3. The Library Club meets on more than once .
4. The mail comes more than once .
5. The storm is over now .
6. The park closes at more than once .
7. I need new shoes now .
8. Our class studies science more than once .
9. Cecilia watches that program more than once .
10. The team practices more than once .

■■■ Finish each sentence. Add the correct form of the verb.

1. I am ||||||||||||||| now.
2. Paula ||||||||||||||| every Tuesday.
3. The cat ||||||||||||||| each day.
4. They are ||||||||||||||| now.
5. We ||||||||||||||| up the river on Sunday.
6. It ||||||||||||||| each Friday.
7. Please ||||||||||||||| on Saturdays.
8. The movie always ||||||||||||||| at 8:00 P.M.
9. She ||||||||||||||| on Friday and Saturday.
10. We ||||||||||||||| a new week each Monday.

Checking Up

Write two sentences that tell about something that happens more than once. Use the present tense.

Write two sentences that tell about something that is happening now. Use a form of **be** and the **-ing** form of the verb.

Adding Adjective-Forming Suffixes

> That snake can be **dangerous**.
> Its venom is **poisonous**.

Read the sentences in the box. Notice the adjectives in color.

- What was added to **danger** to make an adjective?
- What was added to **poison** to make an adjective?

For Practice

■ Add a suffix from the box to make each word an adjective. Write the adjective you make.

-ous	-able	-ful	-y

1. thirst
2. mountain
3. use
4. enjoy
5. break
6. humor
7. hope
8. dirt
9. care
10. storm
11. agree
12. respect

■ ■ Add **-y, -able, -ful,** or **-ous** to the word in each box to make an adjective. Use that adjective to complete the sentence. Write the whole sentence.

1. The child's hands felt stick .
2. The rust key didn't fit in the lock.
3. We left the dishes in the suds water.
4. The girls ran on the sand beach.
5. I feel luck today.
6. The story is laugh .
7. It was a joy time.
8. Everyone was thank .
9. Ed felt hope .
10. That band is fame .

> **Remember**
>
> Suffixes such as -ous, -y, -able, and -ful can be added to some words to make adjectives.

Adding Noun-Forming Suffixes

> Blake has a new **invention**.
> He will add it to his **collection**.

Read the sentences in the box. Notice the nouns in color.

- What was added to **invent** to make a noun?
- What was added to **collect** to make a noun?

For Practice

■ Add a suffix from the box to make each word a noun. Write the noun you make.

-ion	-ment	-ness	-er

1. act
2. climb
3. amaze
4. bright
5. bowl
6. govern
7. predict
8. help
9. sharp
10. teach
11. equip
12. work

■ ■ Add **-ness** to the word in each box to make a noun. Use that noun to complete the sentence. Write the whole sentence.

1. They respect the judge's fair .
2. We could barely see our way in the dark .
3. There is a strong like between Nola and her mother.
4. Carrie chose this material for its soft .
5. Jerry's friendly makes him popular.
6. The fruit's bitter is not good.
7. The steak's tender is perfect.
8. The knife's blunt is a problem.

> **Remember**
>
> Suffixes such as -ion, -ment, -ness, and -er can be added to some words to make nouns.

11
Gaining Library Skills

Libraries have many things to offer. In this chapter, you will learn about some of them. You will also learn how certain parts of a library are organized. You will also learn how to find the book you want.

In this chapter, you will learn

- what you can find in a library
- how books are organized in a library
- how to use the card catalog

183

Using a Library

Looking for Ideas

Look at the picture.

• What different things do the people want to do?

• Where do they all go to do those things?

Talking about Your Ideas

Almost everyone has a nearby library. Many schools have libraries. Nearly every city or town has at least one library.

- What libraries have you been to?

Libraries usually have many kinds of books. They have books of stories and books of facts for people to check out. They have reference books, such as encyclopedias, dictionaries, atlases, and almanacs. You must use these books in the library. But many libraries have other things besides books.

- What other things besides books do the boys and girls in the picture have in their library?
- Which things have you found in a library?

Writing about Your Ideas

■ Read each question. Decide whether or not you might find an answer to the question in a library. Write *library* if you could find an answer there. Write *not in a library* if you could not find an answer in a library.

1. How do fish breathe?
2. When did human beings first land on the moon?
3. When is your mother's birthday?
4. What countries are next to Brazil?
5. Who was the eleventh president of the United States of America?
6. How tall is your cousin?
7. What causes lightning?
8. Who won the last World Series?
9. Who is the youngest student in your class?
10. Which animals hibernate?

■ ■ Imagine you want to find out about each of these things in a library. Decide whether you would use a magazine, a newspaper, a record, an atlas, or a dictionary. Then write *magazine, newspaper, record, atlas, encyclopedia,* or *dictionary* to tell which you would use.

1. You want to know which new cars are best.
2. You want to hear a poem read aloud.
3. You want to know yesterday's most important news.
4. You want to know what *mufti* means.
5. You want to know where Poland is.
6. You want to know how a particular folk song sounds.
7. You want to know what your city council decided in their last meeting.
8. You want to know what states are next to West Virginia.
9. You want to know the population of China.
10. You want to find out when Columbus discovered America.
11. You want to know the birthdate of Abraham Lincoln.
12. You want to know how to pronounce *aardvark.*
13. You want to see what the latest food prices are in the neighborhood.

Checking Up

What things can you take out of most libraries?

What things can't you take out of most libraries?

How Books Are Organized in a Library

Looking for Ideas

Leo is looking for a book. He is having trouble finding it. The books in this library are not in order.

Here's a book of facts about whales. Right next to it is a story book about space creatures. Where am I going to find a book of facts about the solar system?

- What kind of book is Leo looking for?
- Why is he having trouble finding it?

Talking about Your Ideas

The books in a real library are always arranged in order. All the books on the same subject are kept together. This makes them easier to find.

Each book of facts has a code on its spine. This code is called a **call number.** The number tells the subject of the book. The letter or letters below the number tell how the author's last name begins.

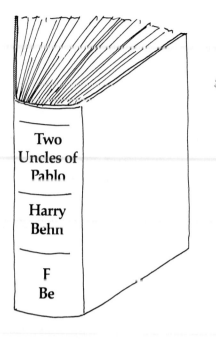

This list shows which call numbers stand for which subjects.

000–099: General works, mostly reference books
100–199: Philosophy and psychology
200–299: Religion and mythology
300–399: Social sciences
400–499: Languages
500–599: Science
600–699: Applied science and useful arts
700–799: Fine arts and recreation
800–899: Poetry, plays, and short stories
900–999: History, geography, and biography

A book-length story does not have a number. Instead, it has an *F* for *fiction.* Below the *F*, it has the first letter or letters of the author's last name.

Look at the books in the picture below. Find the code on each book.

- Which books have call numbers?
- Which books have *F* for *fiction*?
- Which book is about a social science?

- Which book is about language?
- Which book is about science?

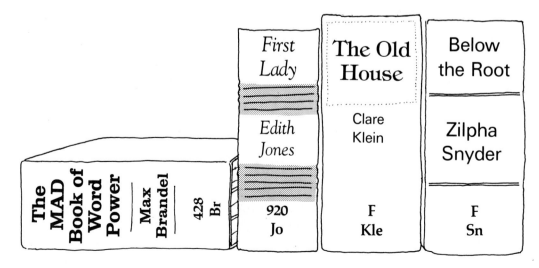

Writing about Your Ideas

■ Look at the books in the picture.

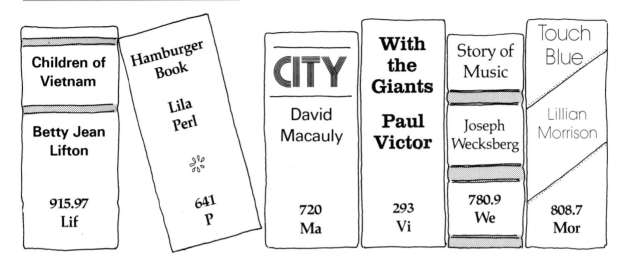

1. Write the call number of each book.
2. Write the title of the cookbook.
3. Who is the author of the book about music?
4. Which book tells about the children of one country?

■ ■ Read the book titles in each group. Write the titles of the two books in each group that should be kept together in a library.

1. *Lions in the Jungle, All about Lions, Explorers in the Air*
2. *Take Care of Your Teeth, Take Care of Your Kitten, Tooth Decay*
3. *Rockets and Missiles, Guided Missiles, Rocks and Stones*
4. *Let's Learn to Swim, Let's Learn to Speak Japanese, A First Book of Japanese*

Checking Up

Read the chart on page 188 again.

In which group of numbers would you find a book of poems?

In which group of numbers would you find a book about the stars?

Using the Card Catalog in a Library

Looking for Ideas

Look at the picture.

What books does the library have about photography?

The answers to all your questions are right here in the card catalog!

Does the library have any books by Eve Merriam?

Does it have a book called <u>The Outsiders</u>?

- What does the boy know about the book he wants?
- What does the first girl know about the book she wants?
- What does the second girl know about the book she wants?
- Where does the librarian tell them to look for the answers to their questions?

Every book in a library is listed in that library's **card catalog.** The cards in the card catalog are in alphabetical order.

Each book with a call number is listed on three different cards. One card is called the **subject card.** It is in alphabetical order by the name of the book's subject.

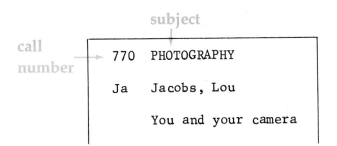

Another card is called the **author card.** It is in alphabetical order by the last name of the book's author.

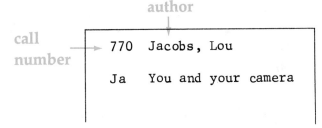

Another card is called the **title card.** It is in alphabetical order by the first important word in the book's title.

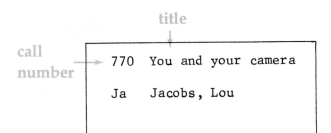

All three cards show the book's call number in the upper left corner. The call number tells where you can find the book in the library.

Each fiction book is listed on two cards. One card is the **author card.** It is in alphabetical order by the last name of the book's author.

The other card is the **title card.** It is in alphabetical order by the first important word in the book's title.

author		subject	
F	Hinton, S. E.	F	Outsiders, The
Hin	The Outsiders	Hin	Hinton, S. E.

Both cards show an *F* for *fiction* in the upper left corner. Below the *F* they show the first letter or letters of the author's last name. This code tells where you can find the book in the library.

Look at these three cards. They are all for the same book.

- Which is the subject card?
- Which is the author card?
- Which is the title card?
- What is the call number of the book?

SOUND		534 Navarro, John G.		534 Our noisy world	
534 Navarra, John G.		Na Our noisy world		Na Navarro, John G.	
Na Our noisy world					

```
    F   Enchantress from the stars

Eng   Engdahl, Sylvia Louise
```

```
    F   Engdahl, Sylvia Louise

Eng   Enchantress from the stars
```

Look at the two cards in the margin. They are both for the same book.

- Which is the author card?
- Which is the title card?
- What is the code for the book?

Writing about Your Ideas

■ Read each of these cards from a library's card catalog. Write the call number or the code that would help you find the book in the library.

```
              CATS

636.8   Rockwell, Jane

Ro      Cats and kittens
```

```
F   Island of the

O   blue dolphins

    O'Dell, Scott
```

```
              MOON

523.3   Kordo, Herbert

Ko      The moon
```

■■ Read each of these cards from a library's card catalog. Decide what kind of card it is. Then write **subject card**, **title card**, or **author card**.

```
              ALPHABET

411   Ogg, Oscar

Og    The 26 letters
```

```
F   Untold tale, The

Ha   Havgaard, Eric C.
```

```
              CHINA

915.1  Rau. Margaret

Ra     Our world: the

       People's Republic

       of China
```

Checking Up

Each book with a call number has three cards. What are the cards called?

Sticking to the Topic in a Discussion

The students in this group are discussing oceanographers.

PARNELL: Oceanographers make scientific studies of the ocean.

HELENE: Some oceanographers are marine biologists. They study the plant life in the sea.

LEON: The plants on our windowsill need water.

LUZ: Other oceanographers study the ocean floor and shoreline. They are the geologists of the ocean.

Read the discussion.

- What is the subject of the discussion?
- Which student did not talk about that subject?

For Practice

■ Read the discussion. Decide which person is not speaking about the subject of the discussion. Take that person out of the discussion. Then write the rest of the discussion.

RAUL: Researchers have been studying dreams. They have found that everyone has several dreams each night.

NICOLE: Usually a sleeping person will have a dream every hour or so.

WALLIE: A person's eyes move during a dream. This dreaming stage of sleep is called REM, for "rapid eye movement."

JANEY: My uncle Ralph's initials are R.E.M.

Remember

When you take part in a discussion, always talk about the subject of the discussion.

Using a Table of Contents and an Index

number
of
chapter →

Contents

number of
first page
in chapter

name of
chapter

name of   pages where
each topic   you can
read about
each topic

The two boxes show what you might find in a book called <u>Yoga and You</u>.

The first box shows the **table of contents.**

- What three things does the table of contents tell about each chapter?

The second box shows the **index.**

- What two things does the index tell about each topic in the book?
- In what kind of order are the topics listed?

For Practice

▪ Use the table of contents and index parts to answer these questions. Write each answer.

1. On which pages can you read about leg stretches?
2. What is the name of the first chapter?
3. On what page does Chapter 4 begin?
4. On what pages can you read about the locust position?
5. What is the name of the second chapter?
6. On which page can you read about a headstand?
7. On which pages can you read about inhaling?
8. On what page does the second chapter begin?

Remember

A table of contents comes at the beginning of a book. It lists the book's chapters in numerical order.

An index comes at the end of a book. It lists all the topics of a book in alphabetical order.

Using an Encyclopedia

Look at the volumes of an encyclopedia. Each has information about itself.

- In what kind of order is the information in an encyclopedia?
- How is a person's name listed in an encyclopedia?

For Practice

■ Imagine you want to find information about these subjects. Write the name of each subject. Then write the letter under which you would look in the encyclopedia.

1. sculpture	10. Walt Disney
2. John Kennedy	11. chess
3. Egypt	12. bowling
4. cattle	13. Italy
5. Anne Armstrong	14. zebras
6. jungle	15. Christopher Columbus
7. Germany	16. Paris
8. John Unitas	17. Igor Stravinsky
9. armor	18. hockey

■ ■ Imagine you are looking in the N,O volume of an encyclopedia. Which of these subjects would you find in that volume? Write only the names of the subjects you would find.

1. ocean	7. Annie Oakley
2. Nevada	8. Richard Nixon
3. microscope	9. New Hampshire
4. Ontario	10. music
5. José Orozco	11. raccoon
6. Orson Welles	12. obelisk

M	N,O	P
12	13	14
Magic to Moon	Nash, to Ogden	Photograph to Potter, Beatrix

Q,R	S	T
15	16	17
Quebec to Rhythm	Saturn to Shakespeare, William	Tallchief, Maria to Tin

Remember

An encyclopedia is a set of books with information on many subjects. Each book in an encyclopedia is called a volume. The information in an encyclopedia is in alphabetical order.

Using an Almanac

The largest mammal
is the blue whale.

The smallest mammal
is the pygmy shrew.

The tallest mammal
is the giraffe.

Read the facts about mammals. These facts all come from an almanac, a special book of facts. The name of this almanac is the *Guinness Book of World Records.*

Read the chapter titles from the *Guinness Book of World Records.*

● Which chapter contains facts about mammals?

For Practice

■ Read each question. Decide in which chapter of the *Guinness Book of World Records* you would find the answer. Write the name of that chapter.

1. What is the largest star?
2. Where is the tallest lighthouse?
3. When was the first bicycle race?
4. What building has the tallest doors?
5. Which planet has the most satellites?
6. Who are the heaviest twins in the world?
7. What plant has the heaviest seeds?
8. What is the highest speed recorded for a skier?
9. How tall is the tallest living man?
10. What is the largest planet in our solar system?
11. Where is the world's longest fence?
12. Which prehistoric animal had the longest tusks?

> Some of the Chapters in the *Guinness Book of World Records*
>
> 1 The Human Being
> 2 The Animal and Plant Kingdoms
> 3 The Universe and Space
> 4 The World's Structures
> 5 Sports, Games, and Pastimes

Remember

The *Guinness Book of World Records* **and other special books of facts are called** almanacs.

12
Changes

In this chapter, you will move and change in many ways. You will be part of a work team, a creature that can take many shapes, and a cartoon animal. As each of the characters, you will react to what others do and how they change.

In this chapter, you will learn how to

- react to changes
- work together to do a job
- be a changing creature
- be an animal character

Doing a Job Together

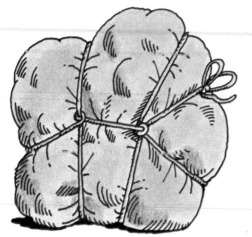

Work with a friend. Imagine you have to carry this package. It is too big and heavy for one of you. You have to work together.

• Look at how the package is shaped. Find a place to grasp it.
• Lift the package from the ground. Move slowly. Remember the package is heavy.
• Walk with the package between you.
• Now you must climb narrow, steep stairs. One of you will have to move backward. Decide who. It is dark. You have to feel your way. Climb slowly. Remember the stairs are steep.
• You must turn a narrow corner. Show how you do it.
• At last you can set the package down. Lower it slowly to the floor.

Working It Out

firefighter
nurse
animal trainer
ice skater
dentist
carpenter
truck driver
artist
basketball player

People do many different things when they work. Read the list in the margin.

• Now you are going to show what each person does.

One person will be the leader. The others will walk in a single line around the room. The leader might name the people on the list. The leader might name people who do other jobs.

When the leader names a person, everyone should stop walking and do something that person might do. When the leader says "walk" everyone should start to walk again.

Acting It Out

You have done things people do when they work. People sometimes work alone. More often people work with others.

■ Work with a group of friends. Choose a job that needs several people. It might be

—performing an operation
—working in a restaurant
—building a house

—running a space shuttle
—playing basketball
—anything else you want

Think about the different things that must be done. Decide what each person will do.

Give each person a number.

Person number one should begin working at the job. That person should make clear movements. Then the others will understand what that person is doing.

Then person number two should start working. Person number two should not do the same thing as person number one. Person number two should do another part of the job.

One at a time, in number order, each person should start doing part of the job.

Work until the job is finished. Sometimes you will be helping each other. Sometimes you will be working alone doing your part of the job.

Talking It Over

Think about what one of the people you worked with did.

How did you know what that person was doing?

What did you do with that person?

Being a Changing Creature

Warming Up

Think about being very big.

- Stretch your arms, neck, and body high up. Now stretch higher, and still higher. Reach out. Take up as much space as you can.

- Stretch your arms, legs, and body wide. Now stretch wider. Spread out. Take up as much space as you can.

- Squat down. Pull in your arms and legs and head. Make yourself as small as you can. Take up as little space as you can.

Working It Out

Look at the picture.

- Tell what is in it.
- Describe how each creature moves.
- Tell how the creatures are alike.

Look at the first creature again. This creature is called Proto. Proto can change into any shape it wants. The other creatures show some of the other shapes.

Imagine you are a creature. You have a job to do. You want to clean and fix up this old house. You can change into different creatures. Think about what each creature can do best.

• Plan the things you will do. Decide what creature you will turn into to do each thing. Remember each creature moves differently.

Show how you fix up the house.

Acting It Out

■ Work with a friend. Choose one of the places in the pictures. If you wish, make up another place. Imagine Proto has come to this place. Decide why Proto has come.

Proto might have come

—to look for something
—to live there
—to meet someone
—to explore
—to build a city
—to help someone
—for any other reason

There is another creature there. This creature will try to stop Proto. Decide what this creature is like. These questions may help you.

—Why is the creature there?
—What does the creature look like?
—What is this creature afraid of?
—Why does this creature want to stop Proto?
—What can Proto do against this creature?

Make up a play about what happens. Decide who will play each part. Plan what you will do. Remember, if you change your shape, you must change the way you move.

Act out your play.

Talking It Over

How many shapes did Proto take?

How were Proto's movements different each time?

How did the other character react to each change?

Being an Animal Character

Warming Up

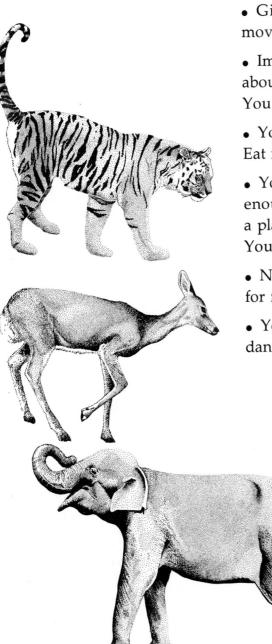

Look at the pictures. Think how each animal moves.

• Give three words that describe each animal's movements.

• Imagine you are one of these animals. Think about the kind of food you eat. You are hungry. You are looking for food. Show how you move.

• You see some food. Move toward it. Take it. Eat it.

• You are still the same animal. You have eaten enough. You want to rest. You look around for a place. Suddenly there is danger! You stiffen. You must get away. Show how you move.

• Now imagine you are a different animal. Look for food. See it. Move toward it. Take it. Eat it.

• You are still the second animal. You are in danger. Show how you react.

Working It Out

Each animal has a special way of moving. You have seen animals in cartoons. The animals move like animals. They don't do the things animals do. They do things that people do.

Look at this cartoon.

Look at the animals in the picture.

- How is each animal still like an animal?

- How is each animal like a human?

Choose one of the cartoon animals. Imagine you are that cartoon animal. You do many things that people do. You still move like an animal.

- You are walking down a crowded street. Show how you walk.

• You see something interesting in a store window. Show what you do.

• You become hungry. You look for a restaurant. You find one and go in. Show how you move.

• You sit down. You look at the menu. You order and eat a meal. Show how you do this.

Look at the picture again. Imagine the animals have a problem. They are trying to solve it. Think about what the problem might be. The animals might

—want to go on a trip
—have to find a new place to live
—want to build a house
—want to form a circus
—do anything else you want.

Acting It Out

■ Work with friends. Choose one of the problems you talked about. Make up a play about it. Decide what will happen in the beginning, middle, and end.

Decide who will play each part. Plan what you will say and do. Remember you are not playing a person. You are playing a cartoon animal.

Act out your play.

Talking It Over

What animal did you play?

What things did you do that people do?

How did the way you move show that you were a cartoon animal?

Reviewing -ing Form Verbs and -n Form Verbs

1. Recognizing -ing **Form Verbs with Forms of** Be
Find the form of **be** and the **-ing** verb. Write the
form of **be** and the **-ing** form verb.

If you need help,
turn to page 49 of your
Practice Handbook.

1. Helen is watering the plants.
2. Harvey and Hal are walking the dogs.
3. Hortense is vacuuming the rugs.
4. Harold is waxing the floors.
5. Hildy and Helga are hanging wallpaper.
6. Hubert is cleaning the closets.
7. The Jumbliks are helping.
8. One Jumblik is washing the sink.
9. The water is spilling on the floor.
10. A Jumblik is mopping it up with a paint brush.
11. The Jumbliks are enjoying themselves.
12. One is painting the walls.

2. Using -ing **Form Verbs with Forms of** Be Add
a form of **be** and an **-ing** verb to each sentence.
Write the sentences.

If you need help,
turn to page 49 of your
Practice Handbook.

1. The cat ||||||||||| her kittens.
2. The miners ||||||||||| picks.
3. The teacher ||||||||||| with chalk.
4. I ||||||||||| the blackboards.
5. Angelo ||||||||||| to the children.
6. Francine ||||||||||| the tigers.
7. Philippa and Jeff ||||||||||| books.
8. Andrew ||||||||||| that bike.
9. I ||||||||||| on the train.
10. Those boys ||||||||||| loudly.
11. We ||||||||||| to the stores.
12. The pilot ||||||||||| the plane to France.
13. Our father ||||||||||| the car.
14. The climbers ||||||||||| to the top.

3. Recognizing -n Form Verbs with Have **and** Has
Find the **-n** form verb in each sentence. Write **have**
or **has** and the **-n** form verb.

If you need help,
turn to page 50 of your
Practice Handbook.

1. The cat has eaten the tuna delight.
2. The moon has fallen below the trees.
3. We have known that all week.
4. The Yankees have beaten the Giants.
5. Percy has broken his arm.
6. The baby has bitten the doll.

7. The crows have flown away.
8. You have grown.
9. The sun has shone on many things.
10. They have gone to the shore.
11. The king has given his word.
12. I have written him ten letters.

4. Using -n Form Verbs with Have **and** Has
Add **have** or **has** and an **-n** form verb to each
sentence. Write the sentences.

If you need help,
turn to page 50 of your
Practice Handbook.

1. The puppy |||||||||||||| just about everything.
2. The wind |||||||||||||| the flowers over.
3. I |||||||||||||| the records to Janice.
4. At last you ||||||||||||||.
5. We |||||||||||||| all we could.
6. I |||||||||||||| a picture of Gerald.
7. She |||||||||||||| the car home.
8. Frank |||||||||||||| this old horse.
9. You |||||||||||||| a mustache!
10. The governor |||||||||||||| everyone's hand.
11. I |||||||||||||| breakfast already.
12. Samantha |||||||||||||| the new plane.
13. Peter |||||||||||||| to the hospital.
14. He |||||||||||||| the medicine.

5. Other -n Form Verbs Find the **-n** form verb in
each sentence. Write **have** or **has** and the **-n**
form verb.

If you need help,
turn to page 51 of your
Practice Handbook.

1. Max has painted the shells.
2. Now I have heard everything.
3. We have called the doctor.
4. He has lost his chance.
5. They have sung that song before.

6. Pete has caught a huge fish.
7. Ella has come early.
8. She has surrounded herself with friends.
9. We have bought the food.
10. Lillian has led the band several times.

13

Combining Sentences

BUILD
YOURSELF
A
GREENHOUSE

Look at the picture. What are the Jumbliks trying to build? What do you think has gone wrong?

The Jumbliks have put together the parts all wrong. Until the Jumbliks put the parts in the right order, they will never have a greenhouse.

You have learned how words and groups of words may be put together to make a sentence. In this chapter, you are going to learn more about how you can put two sentences together to make a new sentence.

In this chapter, you will learn about

- sentences with compound subjects
- sentences with compound predicates
- using conjunctions in compound sentences
- combining sentences with subordinators of time
- combining sentences with other subordinators

Compound Subjects and Compound Predicates

Something To Think About

A loader **arrived.**
A dump truck **arrived.**

The drivers smiled.
The drivers waved.

Read each pair of sentences under the picture.

- Which two sentences have the same predicate?

You can put those two sentences together.
Use both sentence subjects with the predicate.

|||||||||||||| and |||||||||||||| arrived.

Read the sentences under the picture again.

- Which two sentences have the same subject?

You can put those two sentences together.
Use both sentence predicates with the subject.

The drivers |||||||||||||| and ||||||||||||||.

Talking Things Over

The first new sentence you made has two subjects. It is a sentence with a **compound subject.** You can put two sentences together with the same predicate to make a sentence with a compound subject.

● Put the sentences in each pair together. Make a sentence with a compound subject.

1. Hansel recognized the house.
   Gretel recognized the house.
2. The boy crept toward it.
   The girl crept toward it.
3. A robot came out.
   His cat came out.
4. That silver robot ate gingerbread.
   The orange cat ate gingerbread.
5. Gretel looked at them.
   Her brother looked at them.
6. Hansel wanted to ask the robot a question.
   Gretel wanted to ask the robot a question.

The second new sentence you made about the picture has two predicates. It is a sentence with a **compound predicate.** You can put two sentences with the same subjects together to make a sentence with a compound predicate.

● Put the sentences in each pair together. Make a sentence with a compound predicate.

1. Those elephants ate peanuts.
   Those elephants drank water.
2. The bus came.
   The bus left.
3. People greet their friends.
   People look for their seats.
4. The players run on the field.
   The players line up.
5. Bryan catches the ball.
   Bryan runs with it.
6. Al runs after Bryan.
   Al tackles him.

Using What You Have Learned

■ Read each of these sentences. Write **compound subject** if it is a sentence with a compound subject. Write **compound predicate** if it is a sentence with a compound predicate.

1. Archy and Mehitabel sang a song.
2. Abbott and Costello fell down.
3. We sat and waited.
4. They grinned and waved.
5. The fox and the geese went out.
6. They ran and played.

■ ■ Join the sentences in each pair to make a new sentence. If the two sentences have the same predicate, write a sentence with a compound subject. If they have the same subject, write a sentence with a compound predicate.

1. The horse ran across the field.
   The horse jumped the fence.
2. Gloria passed the test.
   Marta passed the test.
3. The baby ran.
   The baby fell.
4. Lions growl at their enemies.
   Tigers growl at their enemies.
5. Porpoises do tricks.
   Seals do tricks.
6. The trainer stands on the side.
   The trainer rewards them.

7. The players crossed the field.
   The players sat down.
8. Letty rolled the dough.
   Letty baked the pie.
9. The mayor made a speech.
   The mayor gave the awards.
10. Jenny lost her watch.
    Jenny found it later.
11. The boys swam.
    The girls swam.
12. The cars went along the road.
    The cars came to a light.

Checking Up

Write two sentences with compound subjects. Write two sentences with compound predicates.

Using Conjunctions in Compound Sentences

• Read the two sentences under the picture.

Molly ran to the bus stop.
The bus didn't wait.

You can join these sentences into one. Use one of the words in the box to join them.

and but or

Talking Things Over

The new sentence you made had a subject and a predicate followed by another subject and another predicate. It is a **compound sentence.**

You can use the words **but, and,** or **or** to join two sentences into a compound sentence. The words **but, and,** and **or** are **conjunctions.**

Read these compound sentences.

We have to hurry, or we will be late.
It is a long trip, and the road is crowded.

• What conjunction joins the two sentences in each compound sentence?

• What mark comes before the conjunction in each compound sentence?

• Join the sentences in each pair to make a compound sentence. Use one of the conjunctions in the box on page 215.

1. They wanted to leave.
   The car wouldn't start.
2. Jake will look for wood.
   Harry will put up the tent.
3. I wish I could help you.
   I'm a stranger here myself.
4. We should go home now.
   Dad will worry.
5. Paul wants to start early.
   John is not ready.
6. Nola will finish weeding.
   Margot will plant carrots.

• Join each pair of sentences twice. Use a different conjunction from the box each time.

1. He likes burnt marshmallows.
   I don't.
2. We should have written.
   She should have called.
3. Becky went skating.
   Norene stayed home.
4. Claud can go now.
   Karl can go later.
5. She likes chocolate cones.
   He prefers vanilla shakes.
6. Peter will heat the water.
   Tina will get the eggs.

Using What You Have Learned

■ Join the two sentences in each pair to make a compound sentence. Use one of the conjunctions from the box on page 215.

1. Andy should be angry.
   He isn't.
2. You had better follow us.
   You will get lost.
3. The king told the queen.
   The queen told the dairy maid.
4. This pie is good.
   The cake is better.

5. Lee wants to go.
   Bert doesn't want to go.
6. Thelma lost the book.
   Rodrigo found it.
7. The plane flew in.
   All the passengers got on.
8. I will go to the movies.
   Maybe I will stay home.

■■ Join each pair of sentences twice. Use a different conjunction from the box each time.

1. I need the money.
   He doesn't.
2. We could paint this table.
   We could build another.
3. We will go to the beach.
   We will go camping.
4. Helga should help.
   Rick should help.
5. I like fishing.
   I also like camping.
6. Stan works on the railroad.
   Steven works in the store.
7. The kittens like to play.
   The cat sleeps all day.
8. Some birds are in their nests.
   Some birds are taking a bath.

Checking Up

Write three compound sentences. Use a different conjunction in each one.

Combining Sentences with Subordinators of Time

Read the pair of sentences in the box. Then read the new sentences made from the pair.

> The crowd cheered. We played.

1. The crowd cheered **before** we played
2. The crowd cheered **while** we played.
3. The crowd cheered **after** we played.

• What word joins the two shorter sentences in sentence 1?
• What word joins the two shorter sentences in sentence 2?
• What word joins the two shorter sentences in sentence 3?

Talking Things Over

after
before
when
whenever
while

Words such as **before, while,** and **after** are **subordinators.** You can use a subordinator to make two shorter sentences into one long sentence.

The words in the box are subordinators. These subordinators all have to do with time.

Read these sentences.

● Tell what subordinator joins the two shorter sentences in each sentence.

1. The baby laughs whenever you tickle her.
2. I'll tie up the papers while you take out the garbage.
3. Tell me your story before you go.
4. I'll tell you when I'm ready.
5. I wrote to her after I heard the news.
6. It rains whenever I forget my umbrella.
7. She will go when she is ready.
8. Amy sings while she works.

Read the sentences in each pair below.

● Use a subordinator from the box to join the two sentences. Say the new sentence you make.

1. I like to sit on the sofa.
   I read.
2. We found your ring.
   We were looking for the spoon.
3. They will feed your skunk.
   You go.
4. Ted visits his cousin.
   They have a cookout.
5. The dog barks.
   Someone comes to the door.
6. Buck left.
   You came.

Using What
You Have Learned

■ Find the subordinator that joins the two shorter sentences in each sentence. Write just the subordinator.

1. I won't leave before you try it on.
2. You should pick up the litter when you go.
3. I feel like laughing out loud whenever I see that picture.
4. I will make some hot chocolate while you take off your boots.
5. We'll put on the records after he goes.
6. I'll be there before you know it.

■ ■ Join the sentences in each pair. Use a subordinator from the box on page 219. Write the new sentence you make.

1. Jenny stayed home.
   Her sisters went shopping.
2. The musicians tuned the strings.
   The curtain went up
3. Everything seems more fun.
   You are here.
4. Nikki arrived at the airport.
   The plane left.
5. The phone rang.
   Frank jumped up.
6. Josh finished his homework.
   He watched television.

7. The road was narrow.
   The workers widened it.
8. Our pilot touched down.
   The weather became worse.
9. We got to the ship.
   It left the pier.
10. They go ice skating.
    They have time.
11. The bus pulled up at the corner.
    The traffic light turned green.
12. Our canary sings.
    He hears music.

Checking Up

Write these sentences three times. Use a different subordinator each time.

Sue listened to the radio |||||||||||||| she read.
Another ship steamed into the harbor |||||||||||||| the first one left.

Combining Sentences with Other Subordinators

Something To Think About

Penguins cannot fly. They are birds.
Penguins cannot fly **although** they are birds.
Penguins are poor runners. Their legs are short.
Penguins are poor runners **because** their legs
are short.

Read the first pair of sentences above the
picture.

- What new sentence is made from the two
shorter sentences?
- What word joins the two sentences in the
new sentence?

Read the second pair of sentences.

- What new sentence is made from the two
shorter sentences?
- What word joins the two sentences in the
new sentence?

Talking Things Over

although
because
if
though
unless

Because and **although** are **subordinators.** The words in the box are subordinators.

- Which two subordinators in the box have the same meaning?

  Subordinators are used to join two sentences

- What subordinator joins the two shorter sentences in each of these sentences?

1. Angelo lost the game though he played well.
2. The *Titanic* went down although people had called the ship unsinkable.
3. The parts of the puzzle will not fit together unless you join them in the right order.
4. A forest fire may start if people are not careful.
5. The fans went home early because they were cold.

You can use subordinators to join sentences you want to put together.

- Use a subordinator from the box to join the sentences in each pair.

  Say the new sentence you make.

1. The hikers kept walking.
   They were tired.
2. Jessie practices every day.
   She wants to be a skater.
3. Your bird will not learn to talk.
   You teach it.
4. Ned is hungry now.
   He just finished eating lunch.
5. You should leave soon.
   You want to be on time.

■ Find the subordinator that joins the two shorter sentences in each longer sentence. Write just the subordinator.

1. I can draw a dinosaur though I have never seen one.
2. Jay won't go to the movies unless his brother comes along.
3. We can skate tomorrow if the pond is frozen.
4. Nora is tired today because she stayed up late last night.
5. The players continued the game although it was too dark to see the ball.
6. The campers knew a bear was nearby because they saw its tracks.

■ ■ Use a subordinator to join the sentences in each pair. Write the new sentence you make.

1. Margo will not go.
   You go.
2. Teddy did not finish on time.
   He started late.
3. Daria cannot go.
   She wants to see the movie.
4. He will go.
   Mother says yes.
5. We could hear the play.
   The actors spoke clearly.
6. Hank could not swim far.
   He practiced every day.

7. The crowd was large.
   The weather was good.
8. She cannot go.
   She finishes her homework.
9. The outing will be a success.
   The food is good.
10. Tina reads one book a week.
    She enjoys reading.
11. The dam did not break.
    It was very old.
12. They will practice.
    We will be at the game.

Write four sentences. Use a different subordinator in each one.

More about Using Commas

Les played the banjo, and Gwen played the guitar.
They asked us to sing along, but we preferred to listen.

The tunes, of course, were folk songs.
Which folk song, Sol, is your favorite?

Read the first set of compound sentences.

- What mark comes at the end of the first part in a compound sentence?

Read the second set of sentences. They have interrupters.

- What is the interrupter in each sentence?
- What mark comes before and after each interrupter?

For Practice

■ Write these sentences. Add commas wherever they are needed.

1. Edwin called for help but no one heard him.
2. The first cartoon was in my opinion the funniest.
3. What program Darlene do you like best?
4. These plants have enough light but they need more water.
5. Mom washed the windows and Dad vacuumed the floors.
6. Lisa was the pitcher and Monty played first base.
7. Your idea Lee sounds interesting.
8. That store is closed but this one is still open.
9. The bus I hope will be here soon.
10. Vicki wants to go skiing but there's no snow yet.
11. Corals look like plants but they are really animals.
12. My sister likes to play tennis but I prefer Ping-Pong.

Remember

A comma comes at the end of the first sentence in a compound sentence.

Commas come before and after an interrupter in a sentence.

- If you need more help, turn to page 9 of your Practice Handbook.

Using Commas with Subordinators

> We'll have our picnic in the park **unless it rains.**
> **Unless it rains,** we'll have our picnic in the park.

Read the sentences in the box.

• In the first sentence, what group of words begins with a subordinator?
• Where is that group of words in the second sentence?
• What mark comes at the end of that word group in the second sentence?

For Practice

■ Rewrite each sentence. Move the word group beginning with a subordinator from the end to the beginning of the sentence. Add a comma.

1. We'll stay home if it looks stormy.
2. Bob peeled the potatoes while Ray cut the carrots.
3. I want to buy some popcorn before the movie begins.
4. Everyone went swimming although the water was cold.
5. We'll have to take the stairs unless the elevator has been fixed.
6. I wear this jacket whenever I go skating.
7. Everyone jumped up when the bell rang.
8. We were all quiet when Carla made her speech.
9. You'll have to hurry if you want to catch that train.
10. We'll be late unless we leave now.
11. Our dog barks whenever someone comes to the door.
12. Rog can't come with us unless he finishes his homework.

Remember

A group of words beginning with a subordinator can come at the beginning of a sentence. When it does, the word group ends with a comma.

◆ If you need more help, turn to page 13 of your Practice Handbook.

People in different times and different places have used these letters and signs to write their thoughts and ideas. You use writing every day. In this chapter, you will learn more about using writing to help yourself and others.

In this chapter, you will learn how to

- write a business letter
- write instructions
- write a book report in the form of an interview
- write a summary

Writing a Business Letter

Manuel wanted to apply for a summer job in a pet store. He wrote this letter to the owner

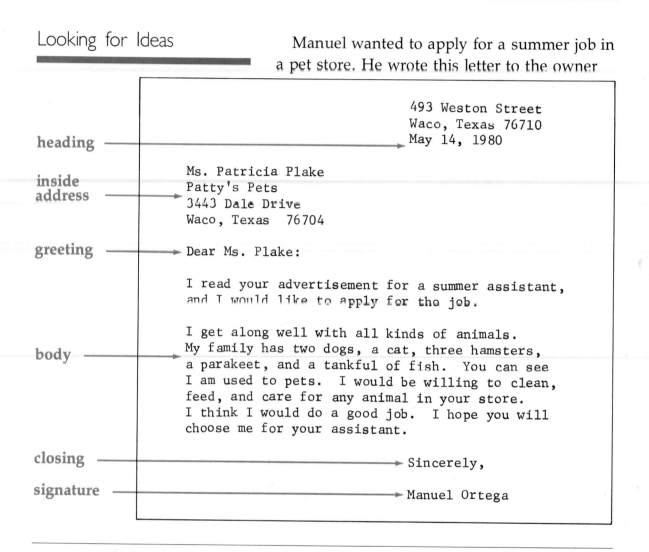

heading

493 Weston Street
Waco, Texas 76710
May 14, 1980

inside address

Ms. Patricia Plake
Patty's Pets
3443 Dale Drive
Waco, Texas   76704

greeting

Dear Ms. Plake:

body

I read your advertisement for a summer assistant, and I would like to apply for the job.

I get along well with all kinds of animals. My family has two dogs, a cat, three hamsters, a parakeet, and a tankful of fish. You can see I am used to pets. I would be willing to clean, feed, and care for any animal in your store. I think I would do a good job. I hope you will choose me for your assistant.

closing

Sincerely,

signature

Manuel Ortega

Manuel wrote a **business letter** to Ms. Plake. Look at the parts of Manuel's letter.

- Where did Manuel write his own address?
- Where did he write the date?
- Where did he write Ms. Plake's name and address?

- What words did Manuel use in the greeting?
- What mark did he use at the end of the greeting?
- What word did Manuel use in the closing?
- How did Manuel sign his name?
- Why did Manuel think he was the right person for this job?

Writing about Your Ideas

WANTED SUMMER HELPER We need a boy or girl to care for our 2-year-old twins this summer. Helper will travel with us and the twins throughout the United States and Mexico. All the helper's expenses will be paid.
Please write:
Mr. and Mrs. Steven Schwartz
P. O. Box 2369
New York City, New York 10007

■ Imagine you found this advertisement in your newspaper.

Write a business letter to Mr. and Mrs. Schwartz. Apply for the job of summer helper. Tell why you think you are the right person for the job.

Be sure your letter has a heading, an inside address, a greeting, a body, a closing, and your signature.

■■ Think of a job you would like to have. It might be a real job near your home. Or you might make up a job you would like to have.

Write a business letter applying for the job you want. Tell why you think you should have the job.

Your letter should have a heading, an inside address, a greeting, a body, a closing, and your signature.

Checking Up

How many parts does your letter have?
Draw a line under the sentences that tell why you are the right person for the job.

Writing Instructions

Ron wrote these instructions for performing science experiments.

> You can perform many science experiments on your own. When everything is ready, follow the instructions step by step. Always begin by reading the instructions for the experiment carefully. Next, get together everything you will need for the experiment. Watch carefully to see what happens at each step in the experiment.

Read Ron's instructions. One of the sentences in his paragraph is out of order.

- Which sentence is out of order?
- Where should that sentence be?

Talking about Your Ideas

You can write instructions. Before you write, think of all the steps you want to write about. Think about the order of those steps. Then write about each step in the order that you must do it.

The sentence in the box on the next page is the beginning of a paragraph of instructions. The four sentences beside the box are the other sentences from the paragraph. But those four sentences are out of order.

• Read the box in the margin. Put the sentences in order.

This experiment shows how heated air reacts.

Next, set the bottle in a pan of cold water.

First, put the open end of an empty balloon over the neck of a small, empty pop bottle.

Watch what happens to the balloon as the hot water heats the air in the bottle.

Then put the pan on a stove and heat the water.

Writing about Your Ideas

■ Read these instructions. Find the sentence that is out of order. Decide where it should be. Write the instructions in order.

This experiment will show you whether air weighs anything. First squeeze as much air as possible out of a football and put the ball on a small scale. Read the scale and write down how much the empty ball weighs. Read the scale again and write down how much the ball full of air weighs. Then pump the football full of air. Put the ball back on the scale. Compare the two weights.

■ ■ Choose an experiment you know how to do. Think about the steps in the experiment in order. Write instructions for it.

Checking Up

Finish this sentence:

You should write each step in a set of instructions in the order ||||||||||||||| .

Writing a Book Report

Looking for Ideas

Sherry read a book called *Over Sea, Under Stone*. Then she wrote this book report. In her report, Sherry pretended to interview one of the main characters in the book.

Interviewing a Story Character

What is your name?
My name is Simon Drew.

What book are you in?
I'm in *Over Sea, Under Stone* by Susan Cooper.

How old are you?
I'm 13 years old.

Where do you live?
I live in London, England. In the book, however, I was with my family on vacation. We stayed near the ocean in a village called Trewissick.

What is special about you?
My family spends a vacation with Great-uncle Merry. He is a famous professor.

What happens to you?
My sister Jane, my brother Barney, and I find a very old map. It tells where a treasure was hidden long ago. King Arthur had something to do with this treasure. With Great-uncle Merry's help, we hunt for the treasure. Some very mean people are also hunting for the treasure. They try to stop us from finding it. We have a very exciting time.

Talking about Your Ideas

Read Sherry's book report.

- What questions did Sherry ask?
- Which parts of the report did Sherry write as a character in the book?
- What does her report tell about the character in the book?
- What does her report tell about what happened to that character?
- What part of her report tells the title and author of the book?

Think about some books you have read.

- Who is the main character in each book?
- What would you ask the main character in an interview?
- What would your most important question be?

Writing about Your Ideas

■ Choose a book you have read. Write a book report about it. In your report, pretend you are interviewing the main character in the book that you read.

Ask the character the first two questions Sherry asked. Then ask at least three more questions. You may use the questions Sherry used. You may wish to make up your own questions. You may wish to use some of Sherry's questions and some of your own.

Checking Up

Read the book report. Underline the parts of the report that you wrote as a character in the book.

Writing a Summary

Looking for Ideas

Read the paragraph in the box. Then read the three sentences below the paragraph.

- Which sentence tells the main idea of the paragraph?

> The early Native Americans hunted buffalo, but they did not hunt for sport. The Indians used every buffalo they killed. They cooked and ate the meat. They made clothing, teepees, containers, and even boats from buffalo hides. They made tools from buffalo bones. Native Americans did not waste any part of a buffalo they killed.
>
> 1. Early American Indians were skillful hunters.
> 2. Buffalo meat tastes good.
> 3. Early American Indians used every part of each buffalo they killed.

Talking about Your Ideas

A sentence that tells the main idea of the paragraph is called a **summary** sentence.

You can make your own summary sentence. Read the paragraph on the next page. Think about the main idea of the paragraph.

● Say one sentence that tells the main idea of the paragraph. Your sentence will be a summary of the paragraph.

> Collies make very good pets. They are large, friendly dogs who get along well with people. Because most collies are smart, they are easy to train. They are strong and healthy. Many people enjoy having collies as pets.

Writing about Your Ideas

■ Read the paragraph below. Then choose the sentence that is a summary of the paragraph. Write that sentence.

> Bears may look friendly, but they can be very dangerous. Bears that have been frightened or attacked will fight fiercely. They have sharp claws which they use to fight. They may also use their teeth. Bears are large, strong animals. They can defend themselves well.

1. Bears can be very dangerous.
2. Some bears look friendly.
3. Bears have sharp claws.

Checking Up

A summary sentence gives |||||||||||||| of a paragraph.

Writing a Friendly Letter

Keith wrote this friendly letter to his pen-pal in Japan

Read Keith's letter.

- How many parts does his friendly letter have?
- What does each part tell?

date ——————————————————————→ January 13, 1979

greeting ————————→ Dear Yasuo,

        I am in the sixth grade at Harriett Tubman School. We go to school from 9 a.m. to 3 p.m. every Monday through Friday. Our summer

body ————————→ vacation lasts from June until the end of August. We also have three other vacation weeks during the school year.

        There are twenty-seven students in my class. Our teacher, Ms. Travino, teaches us all our classes except gym and music. My favorite subjects are science and art.

        Please write soon and tell me about your school.

closing ——————————————————→ Your pen-pal,

signature ——————————————————→ Keith

For Practice

■ Joyce wrote a friendly letter to her pen pal Siphiwe in Senegal. But the parts of her letter are out of order. Put the parts in order. Then write Joyce's letter.

> Dear Siphiwe,
> Your friend,
>   I was so glad to hear that you and your family are coming on a trip to the United States. My parents have promised we can come to New York City to visit you. Please let me know when you will arrive. I can hardly wait to finally meet you!
> Joyce
> November 12, 1978

■ ■ Imagine you have a pen pal named Christina in Sweden. Write Christina a friendly letter about your school. Be sure your letter has a date, a greeting, a body, a closing, and a signature.

◆ If you need more help, turn to page 84 of your Practice Handbook.

Writing Abbreviations

Read the beginning of the business letter in the box. Each word in color is an abbreviation.

```
                              927 Lake St.
                              Evart, Mich. 49631
                              Aug. 15, 1980

Dr. Audrey Davis
2232 Blane Blvd.
Holly, Pa. 86970
```

- How does each abbreviation begin?
- How does each abbreviation end?

For Practice

■ Find the abbreviations in these sentences. Write each abbreviation.

1. They moved from Valley Dr. to Hilltop Rd. last Oct.
2. Mr. and Mrs. Harrera will be here on Thurs.
3. I see Dr. Jones in Jan. and Sept.
4. We hiked along Ridge Rd. last Sat.

■ ■ Write these names of people and streets. Use abbreviations wherever you can.

1. Doctor Yee
2. Mister Knight
3. Doctor Alice Sands
4. Glen Road
5. Seventh Avenue
6. Hampton Street

■ ■ ■ Write the abbreviation for the name of each day or month.

1. Saturday
2. Monday
3. Friday
4. December
5. September
6. February

Remember

Words such as Dr., St., Apr., and Wed. are called abbreviations. Each of these abbreviations begins with a capital letter and ends with a period.

- If you need more help, turn to pages 1 and 5 of your Practice Handbook.

Adding Verb-Forming Suffixes

> The shades **darken** the room.
> Ghost stories **frighten** the children.

Read the sentences. Notice the verbs in color.

- What was added to **dark** to make a verb?
- What was added to **fright** to make a verb?

For Practice

■ Add a suffix from the box to make each word a verb. Write the verb you make. Inform students that they may drop the letter *y* when a suffix begins with the letter *i*.

-en   -ize   -ify

1. deep
2. symbol
3. just
4. hard
5. alphabet
6. light
7. pure
8. magnet
9. fright
10. modern
11. beauty
12. memory

■ ■ Add **-en** to the word in each box to make a verb. Use that verb to complete the sentence. Write the whole sentence.

1. The tailor will short the right sleeve.
2. Then he will length the left sleeve.
3. A long illness may weak the patient.
4. These lamps will bright the room.
5. The marching band should straight its lines.
6. Please help me fast the latch.
7. Exercise will strength that weak muscle.
8. Soft the butter before you use it.
9. The sky began to dark .
10. That bleach is supposed to white clothes.

Remember

Suffixes such as -en, -ize, and -ify can be added to some words to make verbs.

239

15

Places and Settings

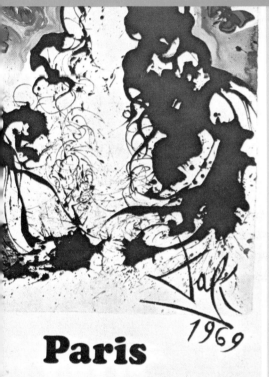

Paris
FRENCH NATIONAL RAILROADS

DENVER

Look at the posters. Choose two posters showing places that are very different from each other. Describe how the places are different.

In this chapter, you will learn more about how to act in a setting. You will also learn how to use a place to help you make up a play.

In this chapter, you will learn how to

- create a setting
- use a setting
- make up a play about a place

Creating a Setting

Imagine you are walking barefoot.

• You are walking on thick, cool grass. Think how the grass feels. Show how you walk.

• You are walking on hot, sharp gravel. Think how the gravel feels. Show how you walk.

• Now you have come to some slimy mud. Think how the mud feels. You slip and slide. Show how you walk.

• Finally you come to a shallow stream. Think how it feels to get the mud off your feet. Show how you walk.

Working It Out

Look at the picture of the valley.

- Name the things in it. Describe each one.

Choose one place in the picture. Do not tell what it is. Think about these questions.

—What can you see in that place? —How would you move in that place?
—What can you hear in that place? —What would you do in that place?

- Imagine you are in the place you have chosen. Show by what you do and how you move where you are. See if anyone can tell where you are.

- Now move to another place in the picture. Show by what you do and how you move where you are. See if anyone can tell where you are.

Acting It Out

Work with a friend. Imagine you have to cross the valley. Plan how you will do it. Think about what might happen. You might

—meet someone friendly   —find a treasure
—meet someone unfriendly   —be in danger
                            —have something else happen to you

Now make your trip across the valley. Show by the way you act the places you are going through.

Talking It Over

Think about your trip across the valley. How many places did you go through? Which place was the hardest to go through? How did you show this?

Using the Setting

Warming Up

Look at the pictures.

• How are the two rooms different?

• Imagine you have to sweep both rooms. Start with the room on the left. You have space to make long strokes with your broom. Show how you sweep.

• Sweep the other room. You do not have much room to move. Show how you sweep around the furniture.

• Now you are going to dust. Show how you dust the first room.

• Dust the other room. You have to work carefully or you will knock over something. Show how you dust the table.

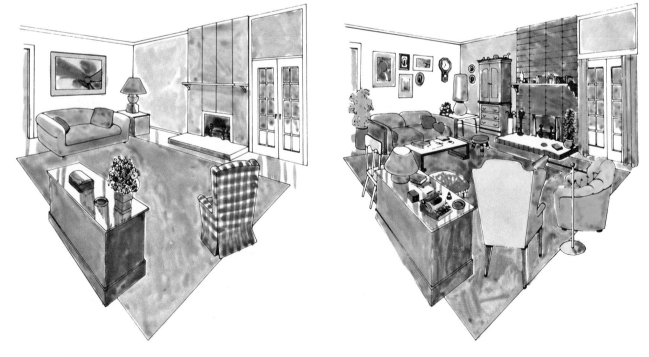

Working It Out

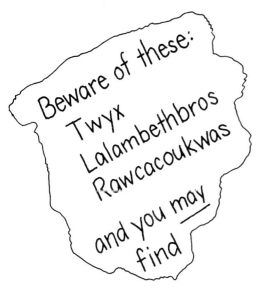

Beware of these:
Twyx
Lalambethbros
Rawcacoukwas

and you may find

Look at the map. It is a map of the valley on page 242.

- What thing is marked in red?

  Read what is on the paper.

- Of what are you told to beware?
- What is missing?

  Imagine you found this map and this paper. You think what you might find could be valuable. Look at the map and paper again.

- Where might you find this thing? Why do you think so?

  You know there will be danger.

- What do you think Twyx might be?
- What might Twyx do?
- What do you think Lalambethbros might be?
- What might Lalambethbros do?
- What do you think Rawcacoukwas might be?
- What might Rawcacoukwas do?

Acting It Out

■ Work with friends. One or two of you have found the map and the paper. You want to find whatever is in the well. You will have to go through the valley. Think of the problems you will have moving there. These questions may help you:

—How long will it take you to cross the valley?
—What will be the most difficult parts of the valley to go through?
—Why will they be difficult?
—Where will you meet the Twyx?
—What will the Twyx do?
—Where will you meet the Lalambethbros?
—What will the Lalambethbros do?
—Where will you meet the Rawcacoukwas?
—What will the Rawcacoukwas do?
—How will you get in and out of the well?
—What problems will you have doing this?
—What problems will you have getting back?

Make up a plan of how you will get to the well. If you wish, draw a map.
Make up a play about what happens.
Decide who will play each part.
Plan what you will say. Plan how you will move through the different parts of the valley.
Now act out your play.

Talking It Over

What things in your play happened because of what the valley was like?
How did the things in the valley help the Twyx, the Lalambethbros, and the Rawcacoukwas?

Making Up a Play about a Place

Look at each color. Choose one.

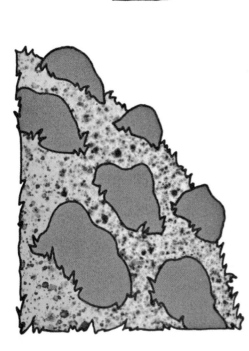

- Name three things that color makes you think of.
- Name five words that describe that color.

Think of the words you have used to describe that color. Imagine you are that color.

You are able to move. Think about the kind of movements you make.

- Are they large or small?
- Are they slow or fast?
- Are they smooth or jerky?

- Show how you move on flat ground.
- Show how you go up a hill.

Now you are going down a steep hill, full of rocks. Think about how you move.

- Do you flow around the rocks or do you jump from rock to rock?

- What other way might you move? Show how you move.

Working It Out

Look at the pictures.

• What three words describe each color? Imagine each circle is a place.

• What might you find in each place?
• How might each place make you feel?

Choose one of the places. Picture in your mind what is in it.

• Move around the place. Pick up some of the things that are there. Show by the way you move what the place is like.

• Think about how the place makes you feel. Show how you feel by the way you move.

Acting It Out

■ Work with a friend. Choose one of the places. Decide what kind of place it is. Decide what things are there.

Decide what in this place could cause a problem. This thing might be

—something valuable
—something dangerous
—something more than one person wanted
—anything else

One of you lives in this place. Decide who you are. These questions may help you.

—Are you a human being, an animal, or an imaginary creature?
—What do you look like?
—Are you friendly or unfriendly?

—Why are you this way?

—Why do you live in this place?
—How do you feel about the thing that is causing a problem?

The other of you has come to the place. Decide who you are. These questions may help you.

—Are you a human being, an animal, or an imaginary creature?
—What do you look like?
—Are you friendly or unfriendly?
—Why are you this way?
—Why have you come to this place?
—How do you feel about the thing that is causing a problem?

Make up a play. Decide what happens when someone comes to this place. Decide how your play ends.

Act out your play. Remember to show by your actions where you are.

Talking It Over

What was the place like?
How did your actions show this?
What was the character like?
How did your actions show this?

Reviewing Sentences

1. Compound Subjects and Compound Predicates
Put the sentences in each pair together. Make a
sentence with a compound subject.

If you need help,
turn to pages 22 and 23 of
your Practice Handbook.

1. Ben ran in the race.
   Laura ran in the race.
2. The doorbell rang.
   The telephone rang.
3. Veronica worked at the science fair.
   Morgan worked at the science fair.

4. Mom read that book.
   Aunt Edith read that book.
5. Elie planned an experiment.
   Rose planned an experiment.
6. The cookies burned.
   The cake burned.

Put the sentences in each pair together. Make a
sentence with a compound predicate.

1. Rover rolled over.
   Rover barked.
2. Tom opened the present.
   Tom smiled.
3. Our class visited a hospital.
   Our class talked with the doctors.

4. Yolanda knitted a sweater.
   Yolanda wore it to school.
5. Cassie weeded.
   Cassie hoed.
6. Hubbard ran toward the fence.
   Hubbard caught the ball.

2. Conjunctions in Compound Sentences Make
compound sentences. Put the sentences in each
pair together. Join them with a conjunction.

If you need help,
turn to page 73 of your
Practice Handbook.

1. Don wrote a long letter.
   Darrel did not answer.
2. Connie heard a noise.
   Paula said it was nothing.
3. Mark likes ice cream.
   Irma doesn't.
4. Dinner was over.
   We did the dishes.
5. Some people came early.
   Other people were late.

6. The actors and actresses were ready.
   The lights didn't work.
7. I went on the trip.
   Cathy stayed home.
8. Lisa works in the store.
   Bob cooks the dinner.
9. The hot dogs were on the grill.
   Mother had bought them.
10. The trip took three hours.
    We were tired.

250

3. Sentences with Subordinators of Time Find the subordinator in each sentence. Write the subordinator.

If you need help, turn to page 74 of your Practice Handbook.

1. Graciela arrived after Mimi came.
2. It rains whenever we plan a picnic.
3. Chuck called his mother before he left.
4. Suzette knits while she watches television.
5. I was not ready when he came.
6. Louise will go whenever you wish.
7. Arthur finished the book before he left.
8. The ants worked while the grasshopper played.
9. Toby gets hungry whenever he thinks of cake.
10. We will visit you after school closes.
11. Susie walks whenever the weather is good.
12. Jim finished before Larry came.

4. Sentences with Other Subordinators Find the subordinator in each sentence. Write the subordinator.

If you need help, turn to page 75 of your Practice Handbook.

1. Cliff went although it was snowing.
2. Trina cannot finish the bookcase unless she buys more nails.
3. I cannot study because it is too noisy.
4. We can start if John is ready.
5. Trish went though her sister stayed home.
6. Warren will buy a bike if he can earn the money.
7. I have read about snakes though I have never seen any.
8. The lights are out because the lines are down.
9. We have a better chance if we work together.
10. Vincent will not make the team unless he practices more.
11. Tasha will not go unless her mother needs her.
12. She will go wherever you tell her.
13. It is cold in here though the windows are closed.
14. Put the cat out because I am going to bed.
15. She did not go although she had time.

16
Relative Clauses

This is the mountain that got in the way.

Read what the characters are saying. What words are in color?

In this chapter, you are going to learn what these words do in a sentence.

In this chapter, you will learn how to

- recognize relative clauses with **who**
- recognize relative clauses with **which**
- recognize relative clauses with **that**
- use relative clauses with **who**
- use relative clauses with **which**
- use relative clauses with **that**

Recognizing Relative Clauses with Who

The girls are proud of their collection.
The girls found the rocks.
The girls **who found the rocks** are proud of their collection.

Read the sentences under the picture.

- How are the first two sentences joined to make a new sentence?
- What word is only in the new sentence?

254

Word groups such as **who found the rocks** in the new sentence are called **relative clauses.**

A relative clause may begin with **who.** Relative clauses which begin with **who** are about people.

- Find the relative clause in each sentence.

1. The magician who entertained us is my uncle.
2. The boys who are on the team came early.
3. The woman who built the machine explained how it works.
4. The girl who waved is my cousin.
5. The boy who answered is Rodney Smith.
6. The man who ate the sandwich was hungry.
7. The farmer who raised the pig took it to the fair.
8. The baby who was crying soon smiled.
9. The people who had come early had to wait.
10. The man who had a key came later.

- Find the relative clause in each sentence. Write just the relative clause.

1. The teacher who spoke to me is Mr. Smith.
2. The girl who found my money is Angela.
3. The man who lives upstairs is a musician.
4. Few who were watching became angry.
5. The girls who wanted to swim came early.
6. Those boys who wished to join had to fill out a card.
7. The students who had volunteered came on Thursday.
8. The pilot who flew our plane is our neighbor.

■■ Eight of these sentences have relative clauses. Write only those eight sentences.

1. The women who work here live in town.
2. The students who had taken the test waited for their marks.
3. The firefighter who put out the fire came from Company B.
4. Those firefighters were tired.
5. The man who had a camera took pictures.
6. The girls who had finished left.
7. The citizens who had come to the meeting spoke to the mayor.
8. Some people came to see Mr. Adams.
9. Many who wanted to see Mr. Adams came.
10. Those who are talking work at Central Hospital.

■■■ Add a relative clause to each sentence. Write the whole sentence.

1. Joe |||||||||||||| is a star on the team.
2. The children |||||||||||||| swam very well.
3. Our father |||||||||||||| fixed the car.
4. The people |||||||||||||| got into the movie.
5. My classmates |||||||||||||| are kind to the younger children.
6. Those children |||||||||||||| are excused from class.

Checking Up

A relative clause may begin with the word ||||||||||||||.

Relative clauses that begin with this word are about ||||||||||||||.

Recognizing Relative Clauses with Which

Something To Think About

Read the sentences by the picture.

• How are the first two sentences joined to make a new sentence?

• What is used in place of **the animals** in the new sentence?

The animals are dead.
The animals lived in these shells.
The animals **which lived in these shells** are dead.

Talking Things Over

Word groups such as **which lived in these shells** in the new sentence are called **relative clauses.**

A relative clause may begin with **which.** Relative clauses that begin with **which** are usually about animals or things.

• Read these sentences. Find the relative clause in each one.

1. The shells which we found are beautiful.
2. The ones which come from there are big.
3. The animal which lives in this shell has a single foot.
4. The shell which was used as wampum was the quahog.
5. The picture which was the most colorful won.
6. The tire which was flat needed to be changed.
7. The sweater which her aunt gave her is green.
8. The plane which just came in is late.

Using What You Have Learned

■ Find the relative clause in each sentence. Write just the relative clause.

1. The gloves which were lost belonged to Roxanne.
2. The meteor which appeared last night was very bright.
3. The paint which you need is on that shelf.
4. The train which came late was empty.
5. The television which is in the family room is broken.
6. The boxes which were empty were thrown away.
7. The package which came today was from Harold.
8. The record which Sally bought was scratchy.
9. The story which you read was written by Juana.
10. The table which is on the porch needs painting.
11. The trip which lasted a month was too long.
12. The song which Seth wrote was beautiful.
13. The truck which carried the furniture was late.
14. The car which I bought uses little gas.
15. The plant which is on the table needs little light.
16. The record which you wanted has been sold.
17. The trees which were cut down were elms.
18. The parks which are closed will be open soon.
19. The pictures which won prizes are over there.
20. The umbrella which is broken is Marcia's.

■■ Eight of these sentences have relative clauses. Write only those eight sentences.

1. The Greeks told stories about many magic creatures.
2. The horse which could fly was called Pegasus.
3. A ram which could speak had golden fleece.
4. The dragon which guarded the fleece was fierce.
5. A horse which had a black mane could speak.
6. The dog which guarded the underworld liked honey cake.
7. A sea monster which ate humans was turned into rock.
8. A chariot which was drawn by dragons belonged to a witch.
9. Some horses could run over the sea without wetting their feet.
10. A horse which had the body of a fish was called a hippocampus.
11. One creature had only one eye.
12. The sirens sang beautifully.

Checking Up

Relative clauses that begin with **which** are *usually* about |||||||||||||| or ||||||||||||||.

Recognizing Relative Clauses with That

The flowers **that the boys picked** were roses.
The boys **that picked the roses** got scratched.
The bee **that stung Leo** was big.
The cars **that lined the road** were all late.
Animals **that live under water** usually do not have fur coats.
The children **that were there** were early.

- What is the relative clause in each sentence?
- Which relative clauses are about things?
- Which relative clauses are about people?
- Which relative clauses are about an animal?
- What word is used at the beginning of each relative clause?

260

Talking Things Over

A relative clause may begin with **that**. A relative clause beginning with **that** may be about things, people, or animals.

• Read these sentences. Find each relative clause. Tell whether it is about people, things, or animals.

1. The boy that was sick stayed home.
2. The rain that we needed finally came.
3. The snake that escaped is poisonous.
4. The tomatoes that were ripe were picked.
5. The things that were lost have been found.
6. The girl that I saw was Charlotte Chinn.
7. The books that were in the library have been checked out.
8. The papers that were on the desk are gone.

Read each sentence.
• What word group in each sentence is a relative clause?
• Which relative clauses begin with **which**?
• Which relative clauses begin with **who**?
• Which relative clauses begin with **that**?

1. The girl that caught this fish feels proud.
2. The fish that she caught is huge.
3. The program which comes next is "Space Creatures."
4. The students who came were polite.
5. The songs which we sang are old.
6. The people that I know are not home.
7. The students who studied passed the test.
8. The streets which have ice on them are dangerous.
9. The plane that took off is a jet.
10. The boy who likes hammering became a carpenter.

Using What
You Have Learned

■ Find the relative clause in each sentence.
Write just the relative clause.

1. The story that Curt told was thrilling.
2. The bus that Cora takes is crowded.
3. The girl who lived there gave us directions.
4. The man that spoke to us lives in our city.
5. Questions that Ms. Stimson asks are hard.
6. The river which flows near town is very low.
7. The girl who sat next to Mona is gone.
8. The house that I meant is down the street.
9. The boots that are muddy belong to Don.
10. The coat which Marla chose is blue.
11. The castle which is on the hill is famous.
12. Six girls who were in class received prizes.

■ ■ Ten of these sentences have relative
clauses. Write only those ten sentences.

1. The school that is on Elm Street is old.
2. The girl that Meg knows is over there.
3. The house needs to be painted.
4. The player who scored points was cheered.
5. The coat which is torn is in the closet.
6. The dog that kept barking is really friendly.
7. Doug Brown lives here.
8. The family that lived there moved away.
9. The woman who came late left early.
10. The meal which was waiting for us was delicious.
11. The person who bakes the best pie wins.
12. The house which you saw is ours.

Checking Up

A relative clause may start with ||||||||||||| or ||||||||||||| or |||||||||||||.

Using Relative Clauses

Something To Think About

Read these sentences.

The polar bear looked lonely.
The polar bear floated by us.

• Join the two sentences to make a new sentence. Make the second sentence a relative clause in your new sentence.

The polar bear ||||||||||||| looked lonely.

Talking Things Over

Think about the new sentence you made.

• How did you change the second sentence to make it a relative clause in your new sentence?

Read these sentence pairs.

• Join the sentences in each pair to make a new sentence. Make the second sentence a relative clause in your new sentence.

1. The house was sold.
   The house had round windows.
2. The ship sank.
   The ship was leaking.
3. The seals do tricks.
   The seals are in the pool.
4. The children laughed.
   The children were watching.
5. The cattle need fresh hay.
   The cattle are in the barn.

6. The path is steep.
   The path goes through the mountains.
7. The house is beyond the gate.
   The house belongs to Mrs. Wilson.
8. The milk is cold.
   The milk is in the refrigerator.
9. The judge is strict.
   The judge is in this court.
10. The locks are broken.
    The locks are on our doors.

Using What You Have Learned

■ Join the sentences in each pair to make a new sentence. Use the second sentence as a relative clause in your new sentence. Begin each relative clause with **which.** Write the new sentences.

1. The parrot has a long tail.
   The parrot is in the cage.
2. The package might come tomorrow.
   The package did not come today.
3. The kite belongs to Alvina.
   The kite flew highest.
4. The book bag is Charlie's.
   The book bag has a broken strap.
5. The snack is for you.
   The snack is on the table.
6. The plant was grown by Ana.
   The plant has many tomatoes

■■ Join the sentences in each pair to make a new sentence. Use the second sentence as a relative clause in your new sentence. Begin each relative clause with **who.** Write the new sentence.

1. Two boys were bitten.
   Two boys teased that parrot.
2. The man was in a hurry.
   The man dropped the package.
3. The girl was not hurt.
   The girl fell off her bike.
4. The woman is our dentist.
   The woman was in the car.
5. The girl started to run.
   The girl was late.
6. The poet will talk to our class.
   The poet wrote these poems.

■ ■ ■ Join the sentences in each pair to make a new sentence. Use the second sentence as a relative clause in your new sentence. Begin each relative clause with **that.** Write the new sentences.

1. The workers worked hard.
   The workers are in the hive.
2. The spaghetti tastes good.
   The spaghetti is on the stove.
3. The bike is mine.
   The bike is by the door.
4. The bird is a woodpecker.
   The bird is in that tree.
5. The beaches are clean.
   The beaches are on the lake.
6. The ice cream is on the table.
   The ice cream is melted.

■ ■ ■ ■ Add a relative clause to each sentence. Write the sentences.

1. The boy ||||||||||||||| is my cousin.
2. The cat ||||||||||||||| belongs to Ms. Strange.
3. The hamster ||||||||||||||| is in the cage now.
4. The sudden shout ||||||||||||||| was never explained.
5. The plane ||||||||||||||| disappeared.
6. The plans ||||||||||||||| were carried out.
7. The stranger ||||||||||||||| speaks to no one.
8. The team ||||||||||||||| finally won.
9. The girl ||||||||||||||| was excited.
10. The boy ||||||||||||||| hurried away.

Checking Up

Write three sentences with relative clauses. Use **that** to begin the relative clause in the first sentence. Use **which** to begin the relative clause in the second sentence. Use **who** to begin the relative clause in the third sentence.

Adding Adverb-Forming Suffixes

> Letty left the room **quickly**.
> She slammed the door **loudly**.

Read the sentences in the box. Notice the adverbs in color.

- What was added to **quick** to make an adverb?
- What was added to **loud** to make an adverb?

For Practice

■ Add a suffix from the box to make each word an adverb. Write the adverb you make.

> -ly   -ward   -wise

1. graceful   5. clock   9. careful
2. quick   6. kind   10. back
3. home   7. west   11. proud
4. correct   8. quiet   12. slow

■■ Add **-ly** to the word in each box to make an adverb. Use that adverb to complete the sentence. Write the whole sentence.

1. The cat meowed fierce .
2. The mice looked around fearful .
3. One mouse spoke up brave .
4. That mouse approached the cat confident .
5. The cat ate the mouse quick .
6. The other mice shouted forceful .
7. The cat purred contented .
8. The cat walked away slow .

Remember

Suffixes such as -ly, -ward, **and** -wise **can be added to some words to make adverbs.**

Using Adverbs

Tasha listened to the question **silently.**
She thought about it **carefully.**
She answered the question **correctly.**

Read the sentences in the box.

- What adverb tells **how** in each sentence?
- With what two letters does each adverb end?

For Practice

■ Choose the adverb from each box. Use the adverb to complete the sentence. Write the whole sentence.

1. Gordie ran up the stairs quiet, quietly .
2. The girls looked around hopefully, hopeful .
3. Jay read the story slow, slowly .
4. Nancy caught the ball easy, easily .
5. Mr. Rodriguez nodded thoughtfully, thoughtful .
6. The bus stopped sudden, suddenly .
7. Bonnie hit the drum firm, firmly .
8. Corliss plays chess skillful, skillfully .
9. We made our decision carefully, careful .
10. The chorus sang beautiful, beautifully .
11. Ms. Jordan spoke kindly, kind .
12. The cats hissed loud, loudly .
13. The people lined up careless, carelessly .
14. The curtains were pulled back swift, swiftly .
15. The performers danced graceful, gracefully .
16. Everything worked perfect, perfectly .
17. The time went quick, quickly .
18. We met them hurried, hurriedly .
19. We are learning to bowl correct, correctly .
20. He petted the dog light, lightly .

Remember

Many adverbs that tell how
end in -ly.

◆ If you need more help, turn to page 66 of your Practice Handbook.

267

17

Writing Reports

You can find all kinds of information in books. In this chapter, you will learn how to organize the information you collect into a report.

In this chapter, you will learn how to

- choose a specific subject for a report
- take notes for a report
- make an outline for a report
- write a report

Choosing a Subject for a Report

Looking for Ideas

Noreen has an idea for a report. She wants to write about Roberto Clemente.

But Roberto Clemente's whole life is too much for one report. Noreen thinks of the different parts of his life.

- What three parts of Roberto Clemente's life does she think of?

Roberto Clemente
as a boy in Puerto Rico

Roberto Clemente
as a professional baseball player

Roberto Clemente
teaching baseball in Nicaragua

Talking about Your Ideas

Noreen's first idea for a report was too general. It included too much.

Noreen used her idea to think of **specific** subjects for a report. Each specific subject was about part of Roberto Clemente's life. And each specific subject included enough, but not too much, for one report.

- What three specific subjects did Noreen think of?
- Which specific subject would you choose for a report about Roberto Clemente?

You can think of a report subject the way Noreen did. First, choose a person you would like to write about.

Next, think of two or three different parts of a person's life. These parts can be specific subjects for reports.

- What different parts of each person's life can you think of?

Finally, choose one of the specific subjects for your report.

- Which part of each person's life would you choose to write about?

Writing about Your Ideas

■ Each pair has one general idea and one specific subject for a report. Choose the specific subject from each pair. Write the specific subject.

1. a. Thomas Edison
   b. Thomas Edison's Inventions
2. a. Emily Dickinson's Poetry
   b. Emily Dickinson

3. a. O. J. Simpson
   b. O. J. Simpson's Childhood
4. a. Thomas Jefferson
   b. Thomas Jefferson as President
5. a. Shirley Chisholm in Congress
   b. Shirley Chisholm
6. a. March Fong Eu as Secretary of State of California
   b. March Fong Eu
7. a. Judy Collins
   b. Judy Collins as a Folksinger
8. a. Billie Jean King as a Tennis Pro
   b. Billie Jean King
9. a. Martin Luther King
   b. Martin Luther King's speeches
10. a. Christopher Columbus at Sea
    b. Christopher Columbus

■ ■ Choose a specific subject for a report.

Start with a general idea. Choose one person you would like to write about. Write that person's name.

Then think of at least three parts of that person's life. Write each specific subject under the person's name.

Finally, think about the specific subjects. Choose the subject you would most like to write about. Draw a line under the name of that subject.

Checking Up

You have chosen a specific part of a person's life.

What other part could you have chosen?

Taking Notes for a Report

Looking for Ideas

Chip is getting ready to write a report on Marian Anderson's singing career. He has read one whole book, a chapter in another book, and two encyclopedia articles. Now he wants to outline his report. He is having trouble remembering what he read.

- Why is Chip having trouble remembering?

- What could Chip have done to help himself remember?

Talking about Your Ideas

Chip needs **notes.** He could have written down important facts from the books and articles he read. Then he could use his notes to outline and write his report.

Chip reread the books and articles. This time he took notes. He read this article.

ANDERSON, MARIAN (1902–   ), is an American contralto who won acclaim in all parts of the world. Conductor Arturo Toscanini said, "A voice like hers comes once in a century."

Miss Anderson was born of poor parents in Philadelphia, and began singing in choirs at the age of eight. Her church concerts attracted attention, and groups raised money for her education. After several years of study and successful concerts in Europe, she returned to New York in 1935 to sing in Town Hall.

Then Chip wrote these notes. Read the notes. Remember that he is planning to write about Marian Anderson's singing career.

famous contralto
age 8—started singing in choirs
went to Europe to study and give concerts
1935—concert in New York

- What are all of Chip's notes about?
- Did Chip copy from the book or write in his own words?

• Did he write in complete sentences or in short groups of words?

Now read the paragraph below. Find the important facts about Marian Anderson's singing career. These questions may help you.

—What award was Marian Anderson given in 1939?
—What did she do to help other singers?
—What was especially important about her joining the Metropolitan Opera Company?
—What was published in 1956?
—What did Marian Anderson become in 1963?
—When did she end formal concert work?

• Tell what notes Chip might take as he reads the paragraph.

In 1939, she was awarded the Springarn medal for highest achievement by a Negro during the preceding year. She also received medals from several countries. In 1942, she established the Marian Anderson Award, a scholarship of $1,000 awarded annually by competition to promising singers. In 1955, she became the first Negro to sing with the Metropolitan Opera Company of New York. Her autobiography was published in 1956. In 1958, she became a delegate to the United Nations. Miss Anderson received the Presidential Medal of Freedom in 1963. She ended formal concert work in 1965.

Writing about Your Ideas

■ Imagine you are getting ready to write a report about Mark Twain's early years. Read the paragraphs below. Write the notes you would take to help you plan and write your report.

> Mark Twain was born in Florida, Missouri, on Nov. 30, 1835. He moved with his family to Hannibal, Missouri, in 1839. Twain later made Hannibal famous when he wrote about it in *Tom Sawyer* under the name St. Petersburg.
>
> Twain's family was poor. The father died when Twain was 12, and the boy left school to become a printer. At first, he worked in Hannibal, principally setting type for his brother Orion's newspaper, the *Journal*.
>
> Twain left Hannibal in 1853. He traveled around the country and held many jobs. He was a printer, a river-boat pilot, and a prospector. In one town, he started writing humorous skits for a newspaper. . . .

■ ■ Read about the person you chose for your report. As you read, think about the specific subject of your report. Take notes that will help you plan and write your report.

Checking Up

Read your notes.

Are they in your own words or the words of the book? Are they complete sentences or short groups of words?

Outlining and Writing a Report

Looking for Ideas

Lori wanted to write a report about Susette La Flesche, who fought for the rights of Native Americans. Lori decided to write about Susette La Flesche's childhood. She read about Susette La Flesche and took notes. Then she wrote an outline to plan her report.

Read Lori's outline on the next page.

Susette La Flesche's Childhood

I. At home on Omaha Indian reservation
  A. Her mother and father
  B. Omaha name—Inshta Theumba— "Bright Eyes"
  C. Languages—Omaha and French

II. At the mission school
  A. Learns English
  B. Wants an education

III. At boarding school in New Jersey
  A. Scholarship
  B. Learns about eastern ways
  C. Essay published in newspaper

- How many main parts does it have?
- How many main parts will her report have?

Talking about Your Ideas

You can plan a report the way Lori did.

Begin by reading your notes. Choose the most important facts from your notes to include in your report.

- What facts about Susette La Flesche did Lori choose?
- What facts have you chosen?

Put the facts that belong together in a group. You should have three or four groups of facts.

- In what three groups did Lori put her facts?

- How many facts were in each group?

Use your groups of facts to make an outline.

Decide what is the main idea of each group. This will be a main idea in your outline. List the facts in each group under its main idea.

Now think about the order in which you want to tell your main ideas and groups of facts.

- In what order did Lori put her groups of facts?

You can now use your outline to write a report.

Writing about Your Ideas

■ Write the outline you planned. Decide which facts you want to use. Then decide how you will organize those facts. Your outline may look like this.

I. First Main Idea
  A. Fact about the first main idea
  B. Fact about the first main idea
II. Second Main Idea
  A. Fact about the second main idea
  B. Fact about the second main idea
III. Third Main Idea
  A. Fact about the third main idea
  B. Fact about the third main idea

■ ■ Use your outline to write a report.

Checking Up

Read your report. Next to the part that tells each main idea, write the numeral that idea has in your outline.

Avoiding Wordiness

Several women took part in the American Revolution as spies, and Lydia Darragh was one of them, and she overheard British officers planning an attack, and so she hid the information about their attack in her needlework and smuggled it out to the American forces, and so with Lydia Darragh's help, Washington's army defeated the British at Philadelphia.

Several women took part in the American Revolution as spies. Lydia Darragh was one of them. She overheard British officers planning an attack. She hid the information about their attack in her needlework and smuggled it out to the American forces. With Lydia Darragh's help, Washington's army defeated the British at Philadelphia.

Read the paragraphs. How was the first paragraph rewritten to make the second paragraph?

For Practice

■ Rewrite each paragraph. Divide each into at least three separate sentences.

1. A honey bee colony is headed by the queen bee, and she is larger and stronger than all the other bees, and so her main function is to lay eggs, but she also keeps the colony running smoothly.

2. Paul Gauguin was a banker until he was 35, and then he gave up his banking job and began to paint, and so he lived for 18 more years as a painter in Paris, and at the age of 53 he sailed to Tahiti, and so the people and places of Tahiti inspired Gauguin's most famous paintings.

3. Our class is going to the art museum to see the Roman statues, and we've been getting ready for weeks, and we have read about the history of Rome, and we've also studied Roman art, and so we are looking forward to seeing the real statues.

Proofreading Your Paragraphs

> One day a rabbit met a huge hippo-
> potamus at the river. The hippo teased
> the ~~little~~ *little* rabbit about being so weak.
> "You'll see," *said* said the rabbit. "I'm
> stronger than you think."

Read the paragraph in the box. The writing in red
shows how you can make changes when you proofread.

- How can you change a small letter to a capital letter?
- How can you add a punctuation mark?
- How can you add a missing word?
- How can you correct a misspelled word?

For Practice

■ Find the 15 mistakes in these paragraphs. Correct
each mistake as you write the paragraphs.

Later that day, the rabbet met an enormous
elephant in the bush. The elephant teased the little
rabbit about being so week. "You'll see," said the
rabbit. "I'm stronger than you think.
The rabbit brought a long rope to river. He tied
one end to the hippo's fote. "You pull on this end,"
said the rabbit. "I'll go into the bush and pull on the
other end. You'll see how strong I am."
Then the rabbit took the other end the rope into
the bush. He tied it two the elephant's leg. "Pull as
hard as you can," said the rabbit. "You'll see how
strong am."
The hippo and the elephant pulled and pulled.
The rabbit stod in the middle. "See how strong I
am!" said the rabbit

18
Making Up
and Acting Out a Play

You have learned many things about making up plays. You can make up a play that has a beginning, a middle, and an end.

You have learned many things about acting a character. Just by moving, you can show

—what kind of person or animal your character is
—what your character's objective is
—how your character feels
—where your character is

You can use your voice to show

—what kind of person your character is
—how your character feels

You also know how to use settings to help tell a story.

In this chapter, you will

- plan a play
- pantomime your play
- add words and sounds to your play

To help you do this, you will use all the things you have learned.

Making Up a Play

Plays have settings, characters, props, and stories.

Here is a setting for your play. It is a deep tunnel that has been discovered in the earth. No one knows where it leads.

Look at the picture of the tunnel.

- Tell what you see.

The tunnel might lead many different places. Here are some of them.

Look at each picture.

- Tell what it shows.
- Where else could the tunnel lead?

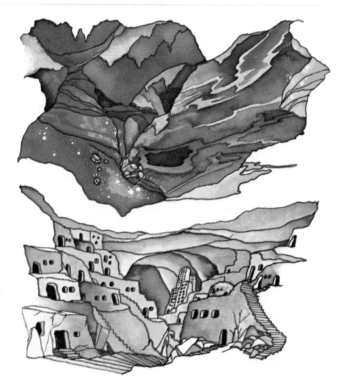

Here are some characters that might want to go into the tunnel:

someone looking for treasure
a cave explorer
a scientist
someone who is running away
someone who sees the entrance while hiking
someone who wants to rest in a cool place
someone who is studying bats
anyone you think of

Each person who comes to the cave has an objective.

• What could be the objective of each person named in the box?

Work with friends to make up a play. First decide these things:

—What characters go into the tunnel?
—What props will they take with them?
—What is each character's objective?
—What problem do the characters have in the tunnel?
—How do they solve this problem?
—What does the place at the end of the tunnel look like?
—What kind of people, animals, or creatures are there?
—What problem do the characters have there?
—How do they solve the problem?

Now plan your play. Plan what will happen in the beginning, middle, and end.

Acting Out Your Play

Decide who will play which part.

Think about the kind of person or creature you will play. These questions may help you.

—What five words help tell what you are like?
—How do you move to show what you are like?
—How do you move to show how you feel?
—How does your voice show what you are like?
—How does your voice show how you feel?

Act out your play two times. First use only pantomime. Then add voices and sounds.

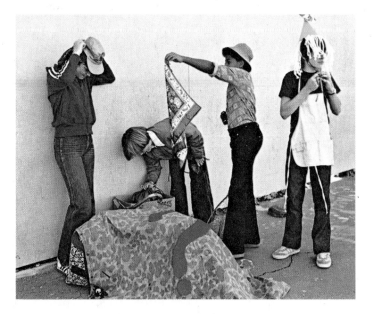

Think about the two times you acted out your play. What things could you tell in words that you could not show?

Reviewing Relative Clauses

1. Recognizing Relative Clauses with Who Find the relative clause in each sentence. Write the relative clause.

If you need help, turn to page 76 of your Practice Handbook.

1. The boys and girls who come here are fun.
2. The people who knew me then didn't recognize me.
3. The man who came to dinner is a spy.
4. Some of the people who come here are lonely.
5. People who don't return books on time must pay fines.
6. Someone who knew the town directed us.
7. The person who is responsible is Mr. Smitherman.
8. Anyone who hadn't studied would have failed.
9. People who go to bed late often sleep late.
10. The woman who called yesterday called again.
11. Those who like to bowl may join the Bowling Club.
12. A person who speaks Spanish is needed.

2. Recognizing Relative Clauses with Which
Find the relative clause in each sentence. Write the relative clause.

If you need help, turn to page 77 of your Practice Handbook.

1. The flowers which you sold me were not fresh.
2. The pencils which the man sold were silver.
3. Shoes which look good are not always comfortable.
4. The bus which leaves at five is crowded.
5. The lock which is on the gate is rusty.
6. The toys which are on the bottom shelf are broken.
7. The package which you sent me didn't arrive.
8. The photograph which I found is old.
9. The work which Sue did is on the desk.
10. The medals which they won are on the table.
11. The bicycles which are at the curb have flat tires.
12. Those animals which have long tails are funny.

3. Recognizing Relative Clauses with That

Find the relative clause in each sentence. Write the relative clause.

If you need help, turn to page 78 of your Practice Handbook.

1. The soup that we ate was more like stew.
2. Everything that you need is in the green bag.
3. The sweater that you like is in the closet.
4. The people that you mentioned are here.
5. The boy that I mean is Josh.
6. The stamps that he collected are valuable.
7. The game that Doreen was in was exciting.
8. The books that you want are out.
9. Those packages that were delivered must be returned.
10. The song that ended the show made everyone cheer.

4. Using Relative Clauses

Join the sentences in each pair to make a new sentence. Use the second sentence as a relative clause in your new sentence. Begin each relative clause with **which.** Write the new sentences.

If you need help, turn to pages 76, 77, and 78 of your Practice Handbook.

1. The seal looked happy.
   The seal was basking in the sun.
2. The jackets were on sale.
   The jackets glowed in the dark.
3. The treasure was raised to the boat.
   The treasure had lain at the bottom of the sea.
4. The plane was a skywriter.
   The plane was going back and forth.
5. The statue was often visited by pigeons.
   The statue was in front of the museum.
6. The mouse was trying to get home.
   The mouse lost its way.
7. Those houses have solar heating.
   Those houses are new.
8. The moon was clearly seen in the sky.
   The moon was orange.

Join the sentences in each pair to make a new sentence. Use the second sentence as a relative clause in your new sentence. Begin each relative clause with **who.** Write the new sentences.

1. People go to the TV studios.
   People want to be on prize shows.
2. People dress up in silly costumes.
   People want to be picked for the show.
3. The people scream and yell.
   The people win cars.
4. The people make faces and stamp their feet.
   The people win jellybeans.
5. Everyone hopes to get rich.
   Everyone goes on the show.
6. Someone lost this ring.
   Someone stopped here.

Join the sentences in each pair to make a new sentence. Use the second sentence as a relative clause in your new sentence. Begin each relative clause with **that.** Write the new sentences.

1. The man had a pleasant face.
   The man sold hot dogs.
2. The boots were lined up on the porch.
   The boots needed polishing.
3. The ketchup wouldn't come out.
   The ketchup was in the bottom of the bottle.
4. The sunlight made a pattern on the sidewalk.
   The sunlight shone through the fence.
5. The scissors are no good.
   The scissors are on the desk.
6. The museum has many beautiful things.
   The museum is on Main Street.
7. The ship docked at the pier.
   The ship needs repairs.
8. The telephone doesn't ring.
   The telephone is on the table.

Practice Handbook

PART I
Capitals and Punctuation

A. CAPITAL LETTERS

Rule 1.

Use a capital letter at the beginning of a sentence.

What kind of lizard is that?
It looks like an iguana.

Rule 2.

Use capital letters in the names of people. Each part of a person's name begins with a capital letter. Use a capital letter at the beginning of a person's title. Use a period after the titles **Mr., Mrs.,** and **Dr.** Do not use a period after the title **Miss.**

Mr. and Mrs. Romano	**Ms. Mae Woo**
Dr. Rivera	**Miss Janice Hancock**

For Practice

■ Write these sentences. Add capital letters wherever they are needed. Add a period to each title that needs one.

1. Here are mr and mrs goldstein.
2. mr waite saw dr pucinski.
3. betty lou phoned miss paxton.
4. we visited ms ki in her office.
5. carla carlton introduced miss louie.
6. dr maxine harmon visited our class.
7. mr ricardo diaz spoke.
8. will ms colette wu come?
9. iguanas are strange animals.
10. have you ever seen one?
11. they remind me of dinosaurs.
12. iguanas may be six feet long.
13. most iguanas are vegetarians.
14. many iguanas live in the desert.
15. other iguanas live in the tropics.
16. several iguanas are in the zoo.

■ ■ Write three sentences of your own. Begin each sentence with a capital letter.

Rule 3.

Use capital letters at the beginning of the names of days and months. The name of each day begins with a capital letter.

Monday	**Friday**
February	**September**

Rule 4.

Use a capital letter at the beginning of each word in the name of a holiday.

Flag Day	**Mother's Day**
Halloween	**Father's Day**

For Practice

■ Write these sentences. Begin the name of each day and each month with a capital letter.

1. Next thursday will be a holiday.
2. Jon's birthday is in july.
3. The team practices every wednesday.
4. These pictures were taken last december.
5. The Smiths are going on vacation in august.
6. Alice visits us every saturday.
7. My brother swims every tuesday.
8. Their club meets every thursday.
9. Two feet of snow fell last december.
10. Our family will go next sunday.
11. These trees usually bloom in april.
12. School year begins in september.

■■ Write the name of each holiday. Use capital letters where they are needed.

1. passover
2. christmas
3. april fools' day
4. veterans day
5. mardi gras
6. valentine's day
7. loyalty day
8. national aviation day
9. lincoln's birthday

Rule 5.

Use a capital letter at the beginning of each word in
the name of a street.

First Street   **Golden Gate Way**
Central Boulevard

Rule 6.

Use capital letters in the names of cities, states,
and countries. Each part of the name of a city,
state, or country begins with a capital letter.

Salem   **Colorado**   **Norway**
New Orleans   **West Virginia**   **Great Britain**

For Practice

■ Write each sentence. Use capital letters where
they are needed.

1. Is burton way far from here?
2. We are moving to los robles drive.
3. Is center street closed?
4. It is closed as far as alanson avenue.

5. There are no stores on claudia place.
6. Is that near placid drive?
7. No, it is near east loring street.
8. That is far from wall street.

■ ■ Write these sentences. Add capital letters
wherever they are needed.

1. Ann was born in poland.
2. Misha visited montana.
3. The farm is twelve miles from great bend.
4. We moved from chicago to baltimore.

5. This plane flies to tokyo.
6. Lisa is reading about greece.
7. The capital of brazil is brasilia.
8. Do they live in rochester, minnesota?

■ ■ ■ Finish each sentence. Use the name of a
street.

1. I live on |||||||||||||||| .
2. My friend lives on |||||||||||||| .
3. A big street here is |||||||||||||| .
4. Our school is on |||||||||||||| .

Rule 7.

Use capital letters at the beginning of every important word in a title. Use capital letters at the beginning of the first and last word in a title.

Words in Titles	
Words That Always Begin with a Capital Letter	Words That Begin with a Capital Letter Only When They Are the First or Last Word
first word last word important words	a and with without the in about to of or for at

For Practice

■ Write each story title. Use capital letters where they are needed.

1. from top to bottom
2. on my own
3. one step at a time
4. swift and sure
5. only once
6. a surprise in the cellar
7. my best friend
8. paula's plan
9. feet on the ground
10. the story of the stars
11. working in a hospital
12. on the mountain
13. the first americans
14. the fiftieth state

Rule 8.

Use capital letters at the beginning of the
abbreviations of the names of days and months.
Use a period at the end of each abbreviation.

Sunday—Sun.   Thursday—Thurs.
Monday—Mon.   Friday—Fri.
Tuesday—Tues.   Saturday—Sat.
Wednesday—Wed.

January—Jan.   July
February—Feb.   August—Aug.
March—Mar.   September—Sept.
April—Apr.   October—Oct.
May   November—Nov.
June   December—Dec.

For Practice

■ Write the abbreviations for the names of these
days and months.

1. Friday   11. Saturday
2. Tuesday   12. February
3. April   13. Sunday
4. November   14. March
5. Monday   15. Thursday
6. August   16. September
7. January   17. July
8. Wednesday   18. May
9. December   19. June
10. October

■ ■ Write the abbreviations for the names of the
months in alphabetical order.

■ ■ ■ Write the abbreviations for the names of
the days in alphabetical order.

B. PUNCTUATION

Rule 1.

Use a period after a sentence that tells something.

   This hat is too big for me.

Use a period after a sentence that tells someone to do something.

   Try on the hat.

Use a question mark after a sentence that asks something.

   How does it look?

If a sentence that tells something or a sentence that tells someone to do something shows strong feelings, use an exclamation mark.

   We're late!   **Hurry!**

For Practice

■ Write these sentences. Use a period, a question mark, or an exclamation mark at the end of each sentence.

1. We're going fishing
2. Would you like to come along
3. Get your fishing pole
4. Are you ready
5. Be careful
6. Those rocks are slippery
7. What kind of bait are you using
8. The fish should like that
9. Tina looks tired of waiting
10. At last I've got a bite
11. Get the net
12. Look at this fish
13. It's huge
14. How many did you catch

Rule 2.

Use a comma after the number of the day in a date.

May 21, 2979   December 1, 1980

Rule 3.

Use a comma between the name of a city or town and the name of a state. Use a comma also between the name of a city or state and the name of a country.

Bismarck, North Dakota   Lima, Peru
New Rochelle, New York   Ontario, Canada

For Practice

■ Write these place names and dates. Use commas where they are needed.

1. Amarillo Texas
2. Gary Indiana
3. Monterrey Mexico
4. June 25 1981
5. February 29 1980
6. January 1 2000
7. Jackson Wyoming
8. Dayton Ohio
9. Nashville Tennessee
10. August 3 1979
11. July 4 1976
12. March 10 1980
13. Calcutta India
14. Juneau Alaska
15. Nairobi Kenya
16. April 20 1990
17. November 12 1982
18. October 31 1980

■■ Write these sentences. Use commas where they are needed.

1. Mr. Butoni flew to Rome Italy.
2. Does this bus stop in Yuma Arizona?
3. Loretta lives in Hilo Hawaii.
4. The Smiths live in Sausalito California.
5. This road goes to Gallup New Mexico.
6. Dory visited Jersey City New Jersey.
7. Alexis was born on July 13 1970.
8. We plan to meet on June 15 1985.
9. This letter was written on May 3 1895.
10. What happened on November 22 1963?
11. Where were you on March 15 1977?
12. They arrived on October 9 1965.
13. People moved in on November 1 1966.
14. The team was formed on May 8 1972.
15. Our house was finished on June 1 1944.
16. This town was founded on July 4 1876.

Rule 4.

Use a comma to separate names in a series.

Lorna, Mack, and Duffy made the salad.
They used lettuce, celery, carrots, and tomatoes.
They served hamburgers, rolls, and beans with
the salad.

For Practice

■ Write each sentence. Use commas to separate the
names in each series.

1. Armando Derrick Jean and Nina went to the
   zoo.
2. They saw gorillas snakes elephants and ostriches.
3. They ate peanuts popcorn and cotton candy.
4. Walter Gwen and Mrs. Penn planted flowers.
5. They are growing daisies zinnias and daphnes.
6. The bus stopped in Augusta Waterville and
   Bangor.
7. Les added pudding eggs and water to the cake mix.
8. You will find paper paints and brushes in the
   cabinet.
9. Bette looked in the attic the kitchen and the
   living room.
10. Our friends brought balloons masks hats and
    horns.
11. I saw Jenny Linda and William.
12. The books papers and pencils are on the table.
13. Soda popcorn hot dogs and milk are for sale.
14. Men women and children crowded in.
15. The zoo contains elephants tigers pandas and
    kangaroos.
16. The street has houses office buildings libraries
    and museums on it.
17. We ate soup salad fish and vegetables for
    lunch.

Rule 5.

Use a comma before the word **and, but,** or **or** when that word joins the two sentences in a compound sentence.

Lonny played the piano, and Lynne sang.
The bell rang, but no one left the room.
We can finish tonight, or we can wait until tomorrow.

For Practice

■ Write these compound sentences. Add a comma to each one.

1. The bus stopped and two girls got off.
2. Eva cleared the table and Nick washed the dishes.
3. We'll have to hurry or we'll be late.
4. The electricity went off and the house became dark.
5. Dad looked everywhere but he couldn't find the flashlight.
6. Blair ordered a soda and his mother asked for a milkshake.
7. Nan likes basketball but Jill prefers volleyball.
8. Mom went to the meeting but Aunt Amy stayed home.
9. I can go with you now or I can meet you there later.
10. The road was narrow and the car was wide.
11. Dina knocked on the door but no one answered.
12. The wind howled and rain pounded against the windows.
13. Nora wrote the note and Ned delivered it.
14. We can telephone or we can write.
15. Take the car or wait for the bus.

Rule 6.

Use a comma after **yes** or **no** at the beginning of a sentence. If a sentence begins with the name of the person being spoken to, use a comma after the name.

Yes, the soup is ready.
No, it doesn't need any more salt.
Laverne, would you like more soup?

For Practice

■ Write these sentences. Add commas wherever they are needed.

1. Yes I can be ready in five minutes.
2. Irene would you like to come with us.
3. Stan watch where you're going.
4. No the plane hasn't taken off yet.
5. Yes it snowed last night.
6. Beatrice please wait for me.
7. No I can't see a thing.
8. No Kip doesn't like monster movies.
9. Yes I thought it was funny.
10. Dave what do you think?
11. Yes the book has pictures.
12. No the phone hasn't rung all evening.
13. Dr. Browning can you come at once?
14. Susan did anyone call?
15. Yes Mr. Johnson called.
16. Linda is the dog in the house?
17. Yes the planes have landed!
18. Paul do you think you will win today?
19. No she hasn't come in yet.
20. Tony please close the door.
21. Yes the doctor is here.
22. Paula put the comma in the right place.

Rule 7.

An interrupter is a word or a group of words that interrupts a sentence. Use a comma before an interrupter. Use another comma at the end of an interrupter.

All the speakers, of course, were nervous.
Val's speech, I think, was the best.

For Practice

■ Find the interrupter in each sentence. Add one comma before the interrupter and another comma at the end of the interrupter.

1. The movie in my opinion was very exciting.
2. The television series however was dull.
3. The solution we believe is simple.
4. The price it seems was too high.
5. The door indeed is locked.
6. The rain I hope will stop soon.
7. Jenny of course brought her records.
8. The answer I think is 2,342⅓.
9. Lea unfortunately could not come.
10. The bus however had already left.
11. The crowd fortunately was large.
12. The play in Greg's opinion was too long.
13. Natalie on the other hand thought it was too short.
14. I unfortunately fell asleep.
15. This plan I know is a good one.
16. The story she feels is too short.
17. We perhaps will keep the books.
18. They do indeed have the ball.
19. The play happily ended early.
20. They sadly are being delayed.
21. He therefore will be early.

Rule 8.

Use a comma to separate two adjectives before a noun.

A tall, friendly woman delivers our mail.
She brought a long, interesting letter.

For Practice

■ Write each sentence. In each one, add a comma between the two adjectives before a noun.

1. The cold wet weather lasted all month.
2. The long heavy coat kept him warm.
3. Kate was eating a big juicy orange.
4. Two soft cuddly kittens hid under the couch.
5. Mom wrapped the large heavy package.
6. The actors waited under the hot bright lights.
7. A long dark shadow fell across our path.
8. That big strong horse ate all our roses.
9. This thick dusty book was on the top shelf.
10. The clown wore a huge floppy hat.
11. He dropped the wet soapy glass.
12. It broke into sharp shiny pieces.
13. The cold wet dog came in.
14. The hot bright fire looked inviting.
15. The man sat in the large soft chair.
16. He took a drink from the tall cool glass.
17. The girls like long funny movies.
18. She got on the slow crowded train.
19. Peter took the steep narrow path.
20. I bought a small furry puppy.
21. The long dark hall scared me.
22. I moved to the bright cheerful room.
23. He had a large colorful hat.
24. I need plenty of hot dry towels.
25. The baby liked the big soft toy.

Rule 9.

The part of the sentence that starts with a
subordinator may come at the beginning of the
sentence. When it does, a comma comes at the end
of this part of the sentence.

When Trina slammed the door, everyone stopped talking.
Although he was tired, Walter couldn't fall asleep.

For Practice

■ These sentences all begin with subordinators.
Write each sentence. Add a comma at the end of
the part of the sentence beginning with the subordinator.

1. Whenever the dog barks the cat starts to howl.
2. Unless something goes wrong we will be
   through soon.
3. After the movie was over we all went to Blake's
   house.
4. When the timer rang Chris turned off the stove.
5. Before Mona spoke she thought about her answer.
6. Before the lights went out no one was
   frightened by those ghost stories.
7. If Clara wins this game she will be the champion.
8. Although Sam looked everywhere he couldn't
   find the book.
9. While we were working our friends were playing
   volleyball.
10. Unless the snow stops the school will be closed
    tomorrow.
11. Before we leave we should call Tod.
12. Whenever you are ready Toby will show you
    what to do.
13. Although Pedro was tired he worked for an hour.
14. If Alicia comes the whole family will be here.
15. When I go nobody will be left.

Rule 10.

Use an apostrophe in place of the missing letter or letters in a contraction.

she is	= **she's**	**they would**	= **they'd**
it is	= **it's**	**is not**	= **isn't**
who is	= **who's**	**you are**	= **you're**

For Practice

■ Read the words and their contractions. Write the contractions. Use an apostrophe in place of the missing letter or letters.

1. could not   couldnt
2. they are   theyre
3. I would   Id
4. we will   well
5. there is   theres
6. are not   arent
7. I am   Im
8. she had   shed

■ ■ Write these sentences. Use an apostrophe in each contraction.

1. Im sure theyll be there.
2. Bonnie couldnt reach the switch.
3. That bus doesnt stop here.
4. Theyve lost their skates.
5. Id say that they dont have a chance.
6. Well call you when were ready.

■ ■ ■ Two words in each sentence can be written together as a contraction. Write the sentence. Write these words as a contraction.

1. I said I would go.
2. They are here.
3. Cloris was not going.
4. Robby is not ready.
5. He will go.
6. Who will help?

Rule 11.

Use quotation marks at the beginning and the end
of a direct quotation. Use a comma after words such
as **asked** or **said.**

> **Ray asked, "Don't all cats have tails?"**
> **Nadine said, "Manx cats are tailless."**

For Practice

■ Write each sentence. Add a comma after **said,
asked,** or similar words. Add quotation marks at
the beginning and the end of the direct quotation.

1. Ginger said I wish I had a cat.
2. Clyde asked What kind of cat would you like?
3. She said I think Persian cats are the prettiest.
4. Roz said I like Siamese cats best.
5. Norm asked What's wrong with alley cats?
6. Rita said Alley cats are often the nicest.
7. Barbara asked Where could we get a kitten?
8. Armando said Our cat just had five kittens.
9. Craig asked Will you keep them all?
10. Armando said We want to give four of the
    kittens away.
11. Lee asked Why don't you take one?
12. Ginger said I'll ask my mother if I may take one.
13. Claudia asked What do you think she'll say?
14. Ginger replied I don't know.
15. Norm said I like your idea.
16. Nancy called Watch out!
17. Linda warned It's dangerous.
18. Cyril explained The weather is ruining the
    crops.
19. Mark thought It would be fun to fly.
20. Nancy inquired Do you have apple pie today?
21. Mother laughed You children are really funny!
22. Father asked Where is the apple pie?

Rule 12.

Use quotation marks at the beginning and the end of each part of a direct quotation.

> **Tess said, "Look at that flock of birds."**
> **"What kind are they?" asked Eric.**
> **"They look," replied Nora, "like pelicans."**
> **"Pelicans are good fliers," said Cory. "They sometimes fly 100 miles in one day."**

For Practice

■ Write each sentence. Use quotation marks at the beginning and the end of every part of each direct quotation.

1. Who, asked Joel, wants to go to the lake?
2. We haven't been to the lake in a long time, said Candy.
3. I think, said Lisa, that everyone should go.
4. Lee said, The bus can get us there in half an hour.
5. Everyone, said Mark, should bring some food for lunch.
6. I want to walk on the beach, said Lola.
7. Swimming, said Donna, sounds better than walking.
8. I hope, said Marty, the water won't be too cold.
9. Maybe we could rent a sailboat, said Will.
10. Does anyone, asked Kim, know how to sail?
11. Nadine does, said José.
12. I think, said Carmen, that Li does.
13. When, asked Alonso, will we go?
14. Let's go right now, said everyone.
15. The large birds, said Paula, are landing on the farmer's roof.
16. We may, replied Mary, go to the library.

Rule 13.

Use a capital letter to begin the first word in the first part of a direct quotation.

"What is a peccary?" asked Angie.
Loren answered, "It is a kind of wild pig."
"Peccaries," said Pat, "live in Central and South America."

For Practice

■ Write these sentences. Use capital letters wherever they are needed.

1. "sloths move very slowly," said Penny.
2. Boris said, "they hang upside down in trees when they sleep."
3. "a sloth," added Manuel, "may sleep for eighteen hours every day."
4. Ned asked, "how do sloths protect themselves?"
5. "their sharp claws," explained Corliss, "are good weapons."
6. "another very slow animal," said Rhonda, "is the tortoise."
7. "when a tortoise keeps moving," said David, "it can travel about a quarter of a mile in an hour."
8. "tortoises are well protected though," said Richie.
9. "a tortoise's shell," said Louise, "is very strong."
10. Maurie said, "tortoises live longer than most other animals."
11. Len asked, "how long do they live?"
12. "let's look it up," said Lois.
13. "that's amazing," said Maurie.
14. "yes," Lois said, "some tortoises live longer than people."
15. "i wish I had one for a pet," said Maurie.

Rule 14.

Use quotation marks at the beginning and the end
of the title of a story.

My favorite story is "Today and Tomorrow."

Underline the title of a book.

I read it in <u>Tales from Near and Far.</u>

For Practice

■ Write these sentences about stories. Use
quotation marks at the beginning and the end of
each title.

1. No Laughing Matter is a funny story.
2. Julian read Fleet Feet yesterday.
3. We read Out to Sea in class.
4. West from St. Louis is a story about pioneers.
5. Coreen likes Surf and Sand.
6. Her sister prefers Skis and Skates.

■ ■ Write these sentences about books. Underline
each title.

1. Lila Perl wrote The Hamburger Book.
2. Have you read Julie of the Wolves?
3. We enjoyed The People of the Plains.
4. Glenn is reading No Way of Telling.
5. Who wrote West from Home?
6. I read Paths of Hunters for my report.
7. My library book is The Lost Treasure.
8. I want to buy My Friend Flicka.
9. May I borrow Born in the Jungle?
10. I need a copy of The Cat Book.
11. I have a copy of The Book of Dogs.
12. I'm reading A Tourist in Italy.
13. We all liked The Secret Cave.

■ ■ ■ Write the title of a book you have read.

PART 2

Grammar

C. SENTENCES

Rule 1.

There are three kinds of sentences. A **statement** is a sentence that tells something.

The pond is frozen.

A **question** is a sentence that asks something.

Do you want to go skating?

A **command** or **request** is a sentence that tells someone to do something.

Be careful.

For Practice

■ Read each sentence. Write **statement** if the sentence tells something. Write **question** if it asks something. Write **command** if it tells someone to do something.

1. What is your favorite food?
2. Turn off the television.
3. Those apples are sweet.
4. Are those books from the library?
5. Wait for me.
6. Who baked these brownies?
7. The high school has a swimming pool.
8. The biggest clown climbed into the smallest car.
9. Please be quiet.
10. Why do leaves fall from trees?
11. Nick's mother works in the hospital.
12. This train goes to Richmond.

Rule 2.

Every statement has two main parts. The first part
is called the **subject.**

>**The clown** ran into the ring.
>**She** performed some funny tricks.

The second part is called the **predicate.**

>**Everyone** laughed at her tricks.
>**The clown** bowed.

For Practice

■ Add a subject to each of these predicates. Write
the sentences you make.

1. _____ climbed the tree.
2. _____ looked under the table.
3. _____ smiled.
4. _____ surprised everyone.
5. _____ enjoyed the show.
6. _____ wants to go to Alaska.
7. _____ worked hard.
8. _____ cannot help.
9. _____ won the game.
10. _____ is in a hurry.

■ ■ Add a predicate to each of these subjects. Write
the sentences you make.

1. That hamburger _____.
2. The bright lights _____.
3. Your new bike _____.
4. Ms. Ramirez _____.
5. We _____.
6. These plants _____.
7. A sudden howl _____.
8. The hurt tiger _____.
9. The fire drill _____.
10. The tallest person _____.

Rule 3.

Some groups of words are sentences. A group of words that is a sentence has a subject and a predicate.

Sentences:	Not Sentences:
We heard a siren.	**heard a siren.**
An ambulance raced past us.	**An ambulance**

For Practice

■ Read each group of words. Decide whether the group is a sentence. Write only the word groups that are sentences.

1. The first story.
2. A dog chased us.
3. Out of the yard.
4. Cecilia laughed.
5. My little brother.
6. The door was locked.
7. Craig had the key.
8. The package arrived yesterday.
9. In the car.
10. Let's call her.
11. Pat fixed the lock.
12. Our good friend.
13. I can go.

■ ■ Read each group of words. Add either a subject or a predicate to each group to make a sentence. Write the sentences.

1. Mr. Malloy
2. sent the letter.
3. sleeps all day.
4. slammed the door.
5. The animal trainer
6. crossed the ocean.
7. This picture
8. Darleen
9. dreamed about clouds.
10. The tallest tree
11. A strange object
12. climbed faster and faster.

Rule 4.

You can put two sentences with the same predicate together to make a new sentence. The new sentence will have a **compound subject.**

Natalie	**ran in the race.**
Homer	**ran in the race.**
Natalie and Homer	**ran in the race.**

For Practice

■ Read each sentence below. Decide whether it has a compound subject. Write only the sentences with compound subjects.

1. Karen and I hurried home.
2. Two police officers visited our class.
3. The paints and the brushes are on the bottom shelf.
4. Dolores and her mother built the doghouse.
5. Janice and Gloria jumped into the pool.

■ ■ Put the sentences in each pair together to make a new sentence with a compound subject. Write the sentences.

1. Two planes flew overhead.
   A helicopter flew overhead.
2. The cars drove onto the ferry.
   The trucks drove onto the ferry.
3. The telephone rang.
   The doorbell rang.
4. Bonnie waved.
   Mr. Louie waved.
5. Annette waited on the porch.
   Her brothers waited on the porch.
6. The lions sounded hungry.
   The tigers sounded hungry.
7. Julius played chess.
   I played chess.

Rule 5.

You can put two sentences with the same subjects together to make a new sentence. The new sentence will have a **compound predicate.**

Petunia purred.
Petunia moved her tail.
Petunia purred and moved her tail.

For Practice

■ Read each sentence below. Decide whether it has a compound predicate. Write only the sentences with compound predicates.

1. The audience clapped and cheered.
2. The campers gathered wood and built a fire.
3. The elephants trumpeted loudly.
4. Bill turned out the lights and went to sleep.
5. The ball soared over the pitcher's head.
6. Felicia swung and hit the baseball.

■ ■ Put the sentences in each pair together to make a sentence with a compound predicate. Write them.

1. The friends looked back.
   The friends waved.
2. One climber stumbled.
   One climber fell.
3. The ice cream melted.
   The ice cream dripped onto the floor.
4. The seal jumped up.
   The seal grabbed the fish.
5. Annette ran up the stairs.
   Annette pounded on the door.
6. The vase fell off the table.
   The vase broke.
7. Sally fixed her bike.
   Sally went for a ride.

Rule 6.

You can often put two sentences together to make a new sentence. You can join the two sentences with a comma and the word **and, but,** or **or.** The new sentence is called a **compound sentence.**

Evan wrote the words.   **Sheila composed the music.**
Evan wrote the words, and Sheila composed the music.

For Practice

■ Read each sentence. Decide whether it is a compound sentence. Write only the compound sentences.

1. We can start now, or we can wait for Jan.
2. Pete's friends went to the movie, but Pete stayed home.
3. Carmelita set up the easels, and Joel mixed the paints.
4. Everyone in the group looked tired.
5. The flag came down, and the race was on.
6. Bernie nodded his head, but he didn't say anything.

■ ■ Put the sentences in each pair together to make a compound sentence. Write the compound sentence.

1. The door was locked.
   The key was missing.
2. Ryan sifted the flour.
   Mandy beat the eggs.
3. Cheryl likes to ski.
   Her friends prefer to skate.
4. The official blew the whistle.
   The players stopped.
5. Roxanne played the guitar.
   Everyone sang.
6. Sue mowed the lawn.
   Tony watered the vegetables.
7. Carol went to the supermarket.
   Nat stopped at the cleaners.

Rule 7.

You can change some statements into questions
by changing the order of the words. Such questions
can be answered **yes** or **no.** They are sometimes
called **yes/no questions.**

    The play was funny.
    Was the play funny?

For Practice

■ Change the order of the words in each statement
to make a yes/no question. Write the question
you make.

1. The bus has left already.
2. The clothes are in the dryer.
3. The game has been delayed.
4. Miss Perkins is their aunt.
5. Leonora will help us.
6. All the drawers were empty.
7. Kittens can climb trees.
8. They are afraid.
9. The hamsters have disappeared.
10. Someone is at the door.
11. The music is too loud.
12. Your friends are waiting for you.
13. Stephanie has left.
14. Lael will sing several songs.
15. Bill can ski well.
16. We are here.
17. The boys will play the drums.
18. Our dog is very sick.
19. Mark was in the gym.
20. I must go now.
21. Nancy will read the story.
22. The library was closed.

Rule 8.

You can change some statements into yes/no questions by adding **do, does,** or **did.** You may also have to change the verb in the statement.

   Sybil builds model airplanes.
Does Sybil build model airplanes?

The girls build model airplanes.
Do the girls build model airplanes?

They built this model.
Did they build this model?

For Practice

■ Add **do, does,** or **did** to each statement to make a yes/no question. Change any other word that needs to be changed. Write the questions you make.

1. The boys need help.
2. Felicia looks happy.
3. The dogs buried their bones.
4. The bus stopped suddenly.
5. Some plants trap insects.
6. The tornado destroyed the bridge.
7. That kitten likes cabbage.
8. The musicians practice every day.
9. Natalie sent him a postcard.
10. Millie and Virginia walk to school.
11. Ducks swim on the bay.
12. Polly plays the trumpet.
13. Roger catches fish.
14. They rented that house.
15. Marla speaks Portuguese.
16. Our cat caught a mouse.
17. The sun sets in the west.
18. Our team plays well.
19. The library needs many new books.

Rule 9.

How-questions, when-questions, and where-
questions can be answered with statements that
have adverbs. How-questions begin with the word **how.**

   How do the dancers move?   **The dancers move gracefully.**

When-questions begin with the word **when.**

   When will they perform?   **They will perform tomorrow.**

Where-questions begin with the word **where.**

   Where will the dancers perform?   **The dancers will perform here.**

For Practice

■ Read each statement. Write a how-question that
can be answered by the statement.

1. The villain laughed meanly.
2. The chorus sang softly.
3. Adrienne drew the picture quickly.
4. Miss Hannah smiled politely.
5. They left the room silently.

■ ■ Read each statement. Write a when-question
that can be answered by the statement.

1. The baby will wake up soon.
2. Uncle Max arrived yesterday.
3. Cindy left early.
4. We should start now.
5. The moon will be full tonight.

■ ■ ■ Read each statement. Write a where-question
that can be answered by the statement.

1. They looked everywhere.
2. They found it upstairs.
3. Phyllis is waiting outside.
4. Ken left the note here.
5. Those cats stay indoors.

Rule 10.

Who-questions can be answered with statements about people. Who-questions begin with the word **who.**

> **Who won the election?**
> **Mrs. Abel won the election.**

For Practice

■ Read each statement. Write a who-question that can be answered by the statement.

1. Bette Davis starred in the movie.
2. Julius took these pictures.
3. June Jordan wrote that story.
4. Nick grew these vegetables.
5. Danielle is the president of the club.
6. Randy will sing the solo.
7. The girls rowed the boat.
8. Tabby drank all the milk.
9. Mother is in the bedroom.
10. The skaters moved swiftly.

■ ■ Read each who-question. Write a statement that answers it.

1. Who is the governor of your state?
2. Who is a good actor?
3. Who is a good singer?
4. Who is a good athlete?
5. Who is the author of a good book?
6. Who is a good cook?
7. Who stars in your favorite television program?
8. Who lives next door to you?
9. Who is the mayor?
10. Who makes good hamburgers?
11. Who likes chocolate ice cream?
12. Who wants to go to the movies?

Rule 11.

What-questions can be answered by statements about things or animals. What-questions begin with the word **what.**

What rose suddenly?
The curtain rose suddenly.

What fell off the stage?
Our props fell off the stage.

For Practice

■ Read each statement. Write a what-question that can be answered by the statement.

1. An elephant escaped from the circus.
2. The moon revolves around the earth.
3. A letter arrived.
4. The chemicals exploded.
5. Sheep grazed on the hillside.
6. The icicles melted.
7. The moon was seen through the clouds.
8. Our ship anchored in the harbor.

■■ Read each what-question. Write a statement that answers it.

1. What made that noise?
2. What broke?
3. What surprised them?
4. What was in the closet?
5. What made them laugh?
6. What is burning?
7. What fell off the shelf?
8. What was outside?
9. What is in the kitchen?
10. What is howling at the moon?
11. What is for dinner?
12. What was that?

Rule 12.

A **sentence fragment** is not a complete sentence.
When you find a sentence fragment in your writing,
rewrite it as part of another sentence.

Sentence: **Two men traveled together.**
Sentence fragment: **Through a dangerous forest.**
Rewritten sentence: **Two men traveled together**
                        through a dangerous forest.

For Practice

■ Read each sentence and sentence fragment.
Rewrite the sentence fragment as part of the
sentence.

1. The two men promised to help each other. In case of any danger.
2. Suddenly they saw a bear. Running toward them.
3. One of the men forgot his friend. And quickly climbed a tree.
4. The other man was left alone. On the ground.
5. The bear was coming closer. And closer.
6. The man on the ground fell down. And lay very still.
7. The bear stood right next to the man. And whispered in his ear.
8. Then the bear left. Without hurting him.
9. The first man came down from the tree. After the bear was gone.
10. Tell me what the bear said. To you.
11. The bear gave me some good advice. About friends like you.
12. He said that I shouldn't trust a friend who won't help me. When I'm in danger.
13. Tell the children. To come in.
14. Put the cat out. In the backyard.
15. Friends like you are nice. To have around.
16. We all need water. To keep alive.

Rule 13.

Two sentences written together as one sentence
make a **run-on sentence.** When you find a run-on
sentence in your writing, rewrite it as two
sentences.

Run-on sentence:
Let's go to the pool, I want to practice the backstroke.

Two sentences:
Let's go to the pool. I want to practice the backstroke.

For Practice

■ Rewrite each run-on sentence as two sentences.

1. Darnell has gone to the store, he wants some chocolate cookies.
2. The actors bowed, everyone applauded.
3. I have to go home now, my father is waiting for me.
4. The television is too loud, please turn it down.
5. Vickie is going to camp this summer, she's never been before.
6. I am learning to play chess, my mother is teaching me.
7. Everyone waited quietly, the strange sound started again.
8. Harriet is in the park, we can meet her there.
9. Be careful, someone may be following you.
10. The path was well marked, the hikers followed it easily.
11. The timer is ringing, the cake must be done.
12. It snowed last night, we can go sledding today.
13. You must drive carefully, the road is slippery.
14. It was cold, Cara put on her sweater.
15. The show ended early, Joan went home.
16. Jake went hiking, he likes the outdoors.

D. NOUNS

Rule 1.

Use the sentence in the box to test for nouns. Any
word that fits in the blank can be a noun.

> **One |||||||||||| is good.**

One friend is good. noun
One happy is good. not a noun

For Practice

■ Use the test sentence to test these words. Write
only the nouns.

1. chair	5. book	9. large	13. apple
2. dog	✗ quickly	10. basket	✗ have
✗ unkind	7. teacher	✗ sharp	15. idea
4. player	8. tree	12. jacket	✗ the

■ ■ Find the noun in the subject of each sentence.
If you wish, use the test sentence to help you. Write each noun.

1. One <u>clock</u> has stopped.
2. This <u>book</u> belongs to us.
3. The <u>cake</u> is ready now.
4. A <u>bell</u> clanged loudly.
5. The biggest <u>candle</u> burned brightly.
6. That <u>candy</u> is too sweet.
7. That <u>glass</u> is cracked.
8. The <u>snow</u> fell steadily.
9. That <u>flower</u> is wilting.
10. Those <u>dresses</u> are on sale.
11. That <u>plate</u> is cracked.
12. Some <u>trucks</u> broke down.
13. Our <u>car</u> is parked outside.
14. Those <u>books</u> are overdue.

Rule 2.

The plural of a noun is usually made by adding **-s** or **-es**. Add **-s** to most nouns to to make the plural forms.

one picture	**one eye**
many pictures	**two eyes**

Some nouns end with the letters **s, ss, z, sh, ch, tch,** and **x.** Add **-es** to almost all of these nouns to make the plural forms.

one bus	**one wish**
three buses	**two wishes**

one peach	**one fox**
many peaches	**some foxes**

To make the plural forms of nouns that end with a consonant and **y,** change the **y** to **i** and add **-es.**

one penny	**one country**
four pennies	**many countries**

To make the plural forms of nouns that end with a vowel and **y,** add **-s.**

one boy	**one turkey**
many boys	**two turkeys**

A few nouns do not change to the plural form by adding **-s** or **-es.** They change in different ways.

one child	**one woman**
many children	**two women**

No change is made to form the plurals of a few nouns. These nouns stay the same.

one sheep	**one deer**
two sheep	**many deer**

For Practice

■ Write the plural form of each of these nouns.

1. friend	4. guppy	7. tooth	10. day	13. story
2. city	5. dish	8. bench	11. cow	14. face
3. kite	6. key	9. moose	12. mouse	15. box

■ ■ Write the plural form of the noun in the box.
Write the whole sentence.

1. Two donkey ran across the field.
2. They were followed by four pony .
3. Three man boarded the train.
4. The trout swam upstream.
5. Those tool are in the box.
6. Four monkey played in the cage.
7. The mouse ate the cheese.
8. The rain soaked the box .
9. Wendy winds watch .
10. Look at those puppy !
11. We watched the race .
12. Those deer are shy.

Rule 3.

Many nouns show ownership by adding an apostrophe and an **-s.**

> **The children's skates are lost.**
> **She borrowed her friend's skates.**

Add only an apostrophe to words that end with **s.**

> **The girls' skates are lost.**
> **They borrowed their friends' skates.**

For Practice

■ Add an apostrophe and an **-s** or only an apostrophe to each word in the box to make it show ownership. Write the whole sentence.

1. That boy jacket is missing.
2. The yard is full of the dogs toys.
3. The children friend moved to London.
4. This boy bike is old.
5. These girls books are torn.
6. A pig tail is curly.
7. We watched the birds nest.
8. The students chairs were in a circle.
9. This plant leaves are often purple.
10. The boat motor stopped suddenly.
11. The kite tail fell off.
12. The bears den was dark.
13. The book cover is soiled.
14. Put the kittens bowl there.
15. The four ships engines are not working.
16. They were found in the giant castle.
17. May I have Bill pencil?
18. The dogs house is in the backyard.
19. The sun rays warm me.
20. The players bats are in the car.
21. Our coach office is down the hill.

Rule 4.

Special names, such as Martin Lopez, are called
proper nouns. Each part of a proper noun begins
with a capital letter.

Albany is the capital of New York.
Julie Nguyen swam across Bass Lake.

For Practice

■ Find the proper noun that is the subject of each
sentence. Write only the proper noun.

1. Death Valley has little water.
2. Louisville was their hometown.
3. Tanya Mumford led the group.
4. Lake Saroya is full of fish.
5. Ripple Road runs by the river.
6. Portland is near the ocean.
7. The Metropolitan Museum has a mummy collection.
8. Metro's Store is the largest in town.
9. France is a large country.
10. Twin Peaks is fun to climb.

■■ Finish each sentence by adding a proper noun.
Write the sentence.

1. _____ was my teacher.
2. _____ sings well.
3. _____ is a big city.
4. _____ taught us a lesson.
5. _____ is a high mountain.
6. _____ is my friend.
7. _____ taught us a new dance.
8. _____ scored three points.
9. _____ just moved onto our street.
10. _____ is a famous singer.
11. _____ can lift one hundred pounds.
12. _____ is president of the club.

E. VERBS

Rule 1.

Use the sentence in the box to test for verbs. Any word that fits in the blank can be a verb.

> **People** ▓▓▓▓▓▓▓▓ .

People stop .   verb
People thing .   not a verb

For Practice

■ Use the test sentence to check these words. Write only the verbs.

1. grow	5. smile	9. cry	13. under
2. into	6. hurry	10. understand	14. shout
3. look	7. these	11. apple	15. draw
4. foot	8. help	12. laugh	16. write

■■ Find the verb in the predicate of each sentence. Write each verb.

1. Their friends like ice cream.
2. They watch television.
3. The animals play in their cages.
4. The zookeepers feed them.
5. The squirrels eat acorns.
6. The students answer the questions.
7. The boys read that magazine.
8. The girls tell jokes.
9. The pilot flies low.
10. The car stops suddenly.
11. Bob types fast.
12. Judy bought the tickets.
13. The storm started yesterday.
14. The birds ate the seed.

Rule 2.

Most verbs change to show the difference between
now and **yesterday.** Verb forms that go with **now**
are called **present tense verb** forms.

> **People listen now.**

Verb forms that go with **yesterday** are called **past
tense verb** forms. You can make the past tense
forms of many verbs by adding **-ed** or **-d.**

> **People listened yesterday.**

For Practice

■ The verbs in these sentences are in the present
tense. Write each sentence. Change the verb to the
past tense.

1. The boats **sail** away.
2. The visitors **ask** several questions.
3. They **order** hamburgers.
4. Twenty people **belong** to the club.
5. The gymnasts **practice.**
6. We **hear** a strange noise.
7. The cookies **taste** sweet.
8. Those boys **collect** stamps.
9. We **enjoy** our art class.
10. The hikers **watch** the birds.
11. The ghosts **disappear.**
12. Yvonne and Bess **wait** for their friends.
13. Norine and Monica **plan** the setting for the play.
14. The boys **practice** for two hours.
15. Mr. and Mrs. Tellman **want** that painting.
16. They **watch** the army approach.
17. Our boats **sail** down the river.
18. Three dogs **wag** their tails.
19. Those clocks **stop** all at once.
20. Their cats **need** extra food.

Rule 3.

Some past tense verb forms do not end in **-ed** or **-d**.
These verbs change in other ways.

The students think about the problem.
The students thought about the problem.

They write letters to their senators.
They wrote letters to their senators.

For Practice

■ The verbs in these sentences are in the present
tense. Write each sentence. Change the verb to the
past tense.

1. Radishes **grow** in this garden.
2. The workers **eat** lunch.
3. Seven people **run** in the race.
4. The campers **swim** across the lake.
5. The dogs **dig** a hole.
6. The students **know** the answer.
7. The girls **fly** their kites.
8. Three people **speak** at once.
9. We **break** our old record.
10. His brothers **throw** it away.
11. Leaves **fall** from the trees.
12. The astronomers **see** the stars.
13. The winds **blow.**
14. They **sell** records.
15. Those closets **hold** many secrets.
16. The people **sing** a pretty tune.
17. These children **take** the books.
18. I **think** the clocks stopped.
19. She **finds** the missing treasure.
20. We **sit** in the first row.
21. The smoke **rises** to the sky.
22. Those bells **ring** in the new year.

Rule 4.

Use the verb form that goes with the subject.
Present tense verbs usually have two forms. Use
one form with **singular subjects.**

The dog barks every night.
The boy feeds the dog.

Use the other form with **plural subjects.**

The dogs bark every night.
The boys feed the dogs.

For Practice

■ Choose the verb form that goes with the subject.
Use the verb to finish the sentence. Write the
whole sentence.

1. The boy ⁞⁞⁞⁞⁞⁞ the room. (clean, cleans)
2. The girl ⁞⁞⁞⁞⁞⁞ across the field. (run, runs)
3. The geese ⁞⁞⁞⁞⁞⁞ in a V-shaped group. (fly, flies)
4. Chickens ⁞⁞⁞⁞⁞⁞ corn. (eat, eats)
5. The tide ⁞⁞⁞⁞⁞⁞ and falls each day. (rise, rises)
6. The frogs ⁞⁞⁞⁞⁞⁞ out of the water. (jump, jumps)
7. Plants ⁞⁞⁞⁞⁞⁞ in oxygen. (take, takes)
8. A human being ⁞⁞⁞⁞⁞⁞ out carbon dioxide. (breathe, breathes)
9. The bell ⁞⁞⁞⁞⁞⁞ every day at noon. (ring, rings)
10. Some gases ⁞⁞⁞⁞⁞⁞ the atmosphere. (pollute, pollutes)
11. Birds ⁞⁞⁞⁞⁞⁞ their wings. (flap, flaps)
12. The flame ⁞⁞⁞⁞⁞⁞ . (flicker, flickers)
13. Which birds ⁞⁞⁞⁞⁞⁞ faster? (fly, flies)
14. That man ⁞⁞⁞⁞⁞⁞ higher. (jump, jumps)
15. Some parrots ⁞⁞⁞⁞⁞⁞ . (talk, talks)
16. The plane ⁞⁞⁞⁞⁞⁞ on the runway. (land, lands)
17. Our plane ⁞⁞⁞⁞⁞⁞ off quickly. (take, takes)
18. The moon ⁞⁞⁞⁞⁞⁞ brightly tonight. (shine, shines)
19. The rain ⁞⁞⁞⁞⁞⁞ the dam. (flood, floods)
20. The horses ⁞⁞⁞⁞⁞⁞ in the fields. (run, runs)

Rule 5.

When a pronoun is the subject of a sentence, use
the verb form that goes with that pronoun.

I rest.	**She rests.**
You rest.	**He rests.**
We rest.	**It rests.**
They rest.	

For Practice

■ The subject of each sentence is a pronoun.
Choose the verb form that goes with the pronoun.
Use that verb form to finish the sentence. Write
the sentence.

1. He .... the gong. (strike, strikes)
2. We .... the plans. (draw, draws)
3. You .... the guests. (meet, meets)
4. We .... the mountain. (climb, climbs)
5. It .... down the hill. (roll, rolls)
6. I .... the soup. (taste, tastes)
7. They .... the song. (sing, sings)
8. He .... the paper. (tear, tears)
9. It .... in the sunlight. (fade, fades)
10. I .... the pie. (eat, eats)
11. She .... the piano. (play, plays)
12. They .... their names. (write, writes)
13. You .... the way. (know, knows)
14. I .... every morning. (run, runs)
15. It .... at this corner. (stop, stops)
16. They .... in the caves. (sleep, sleeps)
17. We .... in the afternoon. (study, studies)
18. It .... up the stairs. (creep, creeps)
19. She .... very carefully. (listen, listens)
20. We .... the man to safety. (carry, carries)

Rule 6.

A verb that is followed by a direct object is called a **transitive verb.**

   We heard the thunder.

A verb that is not followed by a direct object is called an **intransitive verb.**

   We listened.

For Practice

■ Find the verb in each sentence. Write **transitive** if the verb is followed by a direct object. Write **intransitive** if the verb is not followed by a direct object.

1. The phone rang.
2. Clarisse answered the phone.
3. The girls shouted.
4. These fish need food.
5. Rodney pours the milk.
6. Some animals have wings.
7. Everybody sang.
8. The president shook my hand.
9. The bus stopped.
10. Wanda whispers.
11. A crowd gathered.
12. Fred closed the book.
13. Our dog sleeps.
14. The farmers raise wheat.
15. A bridge spans the river.
16. The cows mooed.
17. These trees have leaves.

■ ■ Write three sentences. Use a transitive verb in each sentence. Write three other sentences. Use an intransitive verb in each sentence.

Rule 7.

Many verbs can be either transitive or intransitive.
When a verb is followed by a direct object, it is
transitive.

Everyone played volleyball.

When a verb is not followed by a direct object, it
is **intransitive.**

Everyone played.

For Practice

■ Each of these sentences has a transitive verb.
Change the sentence to make the verb intransitive.
Write the new sentence.

1. The players obeyed the rules.
2. The artist painted our picture.
3. Mr. and Mrs. Jackson moved the table.
4. Our team lost the game.
5. The chorus sang three songs.
6. Sara's brother hid her shoes.
7. Nobody understood the problem.
8. Carol won a prize.
9. Mrs. McSweeney drives the bus.
10. The boys watched the game.
11. Corky answered my question.
12. Dad helped us.

■ ■ Use the following verbs in two sentences. In
one sentence, make the verb transitive. In the
other sentence, make the verb intransitive.

1. rides
2. loses
3. writes
4. plays
5. teaches

Rule 8.

Some sentences have direct objects. A **direct object** is a word or a group of words after a verb that is not **be**. A **determiner with a noun** may be a direct object.

   The rescue party found the boy.

A **proper noun** may also be a direct object.

   The rescue party found Bob.

For Practice

■ These sentences all have direct objects. Write the direct object in each sentence.

1. We met Mr. Wou.
2. Fran enjoyed that book.
3. Greg told a story.
4. Everyone likes Debby.
5. Mrs. Walters teaches that class.
6. I visited Sasha.
7. Pat washed the dishes.
8. Naomi wove this rug.
9. Buffy caught the ball.
10. The class finished the mural.

■ ■ Add a direct object to each sentence. Write the sentences.

1. Tyrone knows ⬚⬚⬚⬚⬚.
2. Beth liked ⬚⬚⬚⬚⬚.
3. My friends made ⬚⬚⬚⬚⬚.
4. Thelma told ⬚⬚⬚⬚⬚.
5. Hal wanted ⬚⬚⬚⬚⬚.
6. Rachael helped ⬚⬚⬚⬚⬚.
7. Diego saw ⬚⬚⬚⬚⬚.
8. Irv knows ⬚⬚⬚⬚⬚.
9. They cooked ⬚⬚⬚⬚⬚.

Rule 9.

A **direct object** is a word or a group of words after a verb that is not **be.** Each **pronoun** in the box may be a direct object.

me	you	him	her	it	them	us

Animals like me.

For Practice

■ These sentences all have pronouns as direct objects. Write the direct object in each sentence.

1. Lou lost it.
2. Mandy's father helped them.
3. Ms. Wainwright called him.
4. Everyone followed her.
5. Roxanne asked you.
6. The idea excited us.
7. Mrs. Lopez helped me.
8. Our dogs love you.

■ ■ Add a direct object to each sentence. Use a different pronoun in each sentence. Write the sentences.

1. The puppy licked ⬚⬚⬚⬚ .
2. I like ⬚⬚⬚⬚ .
3. Someone helped ⬚⬚⬚⬚ .
4. Scott heard ⬚⬚⬚⬚ .
5. The story bored ⬚⬚⬚⬚ .
6. The teacher saw ⬚⬚⬚⬚ .
7. The children drew ⬚⬚⬚⬚ .
8. Mrs. Grant saw ⬚⬚⬚⬚ .
9. The fire burned ⬚⬚⬚⬚ .

■ ■ ■ Write three sentences. Use a pronoun as a direct object in each one.

Rule 10.

Be is a special verb. It has three present tense forms. The present tense forms of **be** are **am, is,** and **are.** Use the form that goes with the subject of the sentence.

> **Susan is ready.**
> **The girls are ready.**
> **I am ready.**
> **He is ready.**
> **They are ready.**
> **You are ready.**
> **It is ready.**

For Practice

■ Add a present tense form of **be** to each sentence. Choose the form that goes with the subject of the sentence. Write the whole sentence.

1. The airplane ┊┊┊┊┊ big.
2. He ┊┊┊┊┊ at work.
3. It ┊┊┊┊┊ in the cupboard.
4. The boys ┊┊┊┊┊ on their way to the game.
5. Sally ┊┊┊┊┊ the president of our club.
6. I ┊┊┊┊┊ on the stage.
7. You ┊┊┊┊┊ among those chosen.
8. They ┊┊┊┊┊ on the playing field.
9. I ┊┊┊┊┊ a good student.
10. She ┊┊┊┊┊ the winner.
11. Luz ┊┊┊┊┊ my friend.
12. They ┊┊┊┊┊ happy.
13. We ┊┊┊┊┊ sad.
14. These gifts ┊┊┊┊┊ lovely.
15. The food ┊┊┊┊┊ good.

■ ■ Write three sentences. Use a different present tense form of **be** in each one.

Rule 11.

Be is a special verb. **Be** has two past tense forms.
They àre **was** and **were.** Use the form that goes with
the subject of the sentence.

Tom was ready.
The boys were ready.
I was ready.
She was ready.
They were ready.
You were ready.
It was ready.

For Practice

■ Add a past tense form of **be** to each sentence.
Choose the form that goes with the subject of the
sentence. Write the sentence.

1. The boys |||||||||||| in the garden.
2. It |||||||||||| hot.
3. The work |||||||||||| hard.
4. They |||||||||||| thirsty.
5. The lemonade |||||||||||| cold.
6. Soon the pitcher |||||||||||| empty.
7. The women |||||||||||| on the bus.
8. Some students |||||||||||| late.
9. A library |||||||||||| only a block away.
10. Many stores |||||||||||| near.
11. Mr. Loring |||||||||||| not sure.
12. A snake |||||||||||| under the bush.
13. The children |||||||||||| ready.
14. Our coach |||||||||||| in the gym.
15. The museum |||||||||||| closed.
16. These rocks |||||||||||| heavy.

■■ Write two sentences. Use a different past tense
form of **be** in each.

Rule 12.

A **completer** is a word or a group of words that follows a form of **be.** A completer may be a **determiner** with a **noun.**

That insect is a spider.

A completer may be a **noun** alone.

Those insects are spiders.

For Practice

■ The verb in each of these sentences is a form of **be.** Write the completer from each sentence. Then write **determiner and noun** if the completer is a determiner with a noun. Write **noun** if the completer is a noun alone.

1. Miss Crandon was the winner.
2. Their mother is an accountant.
3. My friend is a clown.
4. These flowers are roses.
5. Uncle Andrew is a teacher.
6. Those people were farmers.
7. Tim and Armando are friends.
8. My snack was an apple.

■ ■ Finish each sentence according to the directions in the box.

1. That animal is determiner and noun .
2. These plants are noun .
3. Ms. Spivach is determiner and noun .
4. We are noun .
5. Those men are noun .
6. I am determiner and noun .
7. They are noun .
8. We heard determiner and noun .
9. Their invention was determiner and noun .

Rule 13.

Use **is** or **was** after **there** in sentences about one person or thing.

There is one teacher with them.
There was a can of soup left.

Use **are** or **were** after **there** in sentences about more than one person or thing.

There are three teachers with them.
There were several cans of soup left.

For Practice

■ Write these sentences. Use **is** or **are** to finish each sentence.

1. There |||||||||||||| four cookies left.
2. There |||||||||||||| a shoe under the bed.
3. There |||||||||||||| one page missing.
4. There |||||||||||||| pencils in the top drawer.
5. There |||||||||||||| dark clouds overhead.
6. There |||||||||||||| some packages for you.
7. There |||||||||||||| a baseball diamond in the park.
8. There |||||||||||||| a job to do.

■ ■ Write these sentences. Use **was** or **were** to finish each sentence.

1. There |||||||||||||| five people in the room.
2. There |||||||||||||| three oranges.
3. There |||||||||||||| a magazine on the floor.
4. There |||||||||||||| a pony in the corral.
5. There |||||||||||||| one banana left.
6. There |||||||||||||| two letters in the mailbox.
7. There |||||||||||||| many things to do.
8. There |||||||||||||| one plane on the runway.
9. There |||||||||||||| many books in the library.
10. There |||||||||||||| too many spices in the food.

Rule 14.

Use -**ing** form verbs after a form of **be.** The -**ing** form verbs usually end with the letters **ing.**

We walk along the beach.
We are walking along the beach.

The tide goes out.
The tide is going out.

For Practice

■ Use the -**ing** form verb in the box to finish each sentence. Write the sentence.

1. Pippa was watch television.
2. Mom is sleep in the hammock.
3. The flowers are bloom .
4. The actors are rehearse their parts.
5. The ship is sail out of the harbor.
6. We were do our best.
7. Shane was write a letter.
8. The scientists are perform an experiment.
9. Les and I are cook dinner tonight.
10. The kitten was purr .
11. This spider is spin a web.
12. The students were take notes.
13. Maureen is work in the darkroom.
14. The rice is burn .
15. How quickly Anny is learn .
16. The castle was glow with candles.
17. The dancers are waltz around the room.
18. The tailor is sew the coat.
19. Those people are sell cookies.
20. These snails are eat the flowers.
21. Our fire is smoke up the camp.
22. We are go today.
23. The keeper is feed the animals.

Rule 15.

Use **-n** form verbs after **have** or **has.** The **-n** form
verbs often end with the letter **n.**

I hide my diary.
I have hidden my diary.

I forget the hiding place.
I have forgotten the hiding place.

For Practice

■ Use the **-n** form of the verb in the box to finish
each sentence. Write the sentence.

1. Cheryl has speak to him.
2. Four inches of snow has fall .
3. I have ride this horse before.
4. Someone has eat my sandwich.
5. A full moon has rise .
6. Ms. Sommers has drive the bus.
7. The water in the puddles has freeze .
8. Vanessa has see that movie.
9. Archie has write a good report.
10. You have break your promise.
11. That remark has give me an idea.
12. Our club has choose a new name.
13. Coreen has take my coat.
14. The kittens have eat their dinner.
15. The papers have blow away.
16. She has bite into the peach.
17. Tad's face has swell .
18. The pirates have steal the jewels.
19. They have hide the treasure.
20. He has forgive him.

Rule 16.

Some **-n** form verbs do not end with the letter **n**.
Use these **-n** form verbs after **have** and **has**.

    The dog jumps over the fence.
    The dog has jumped over the fence.

    The sun set.
    The sun has set.

For Practice

■ Use the **-n** form verb in the box to finish each
sentence. Write the whole sentence.

1. The hikers have walk across the field.
2. They have hike up the hill.
3. Finally they had climb the mountain.
4. They had rest at the top.
5. The firefighters have put out the fire.
6. The phone has ring .
7. Chuck has swim across this lake.
8. He has teach swimming.
9. Stephanie has leave the party early.
10. Toby has drink all the milk.
11. The chorus has sing three songs already.
12. We have finish everything we could.
13. The game has end .
14. Our team has drop the ball.
15. The old rowboat has sink .
16. The children have slide down the hill.
17. The doctors have examine me.
18. Those animals have lose their way.
19. Everyone has read that book.
20. The musicians have play in the parade.
21. I have sign the letter.
22. She has build a large plane model.

Rule 17.

Does and **Do; Doesn't** and **Don't**

Use **does** or **doesn't** in sentences about only one person or thing.

> **The big seal does perform tricks.**
> **The little seal doesn't perform tricks.**

Use **do** or **don't** in sentences about more than one person or thing.

> **The big seals do perform tricks.**
> **The little seals don't perform tricks.**

For Practice

■ Write these sentences. Use **does** or **do** to finish each sentence.

1. The boys ||||||||||||| need help.
2. The sun ||||||||||||| feel good.
3. Your friends ||||||||||||| look happy.
4. Mr. Dobbins ||||||||||||| understand our problem.
5. This cake ||||||||||||| taste good.
6. Gina ||||||||||||| know Patti.
7. Pilar ||||||||||||| know how to play chess.
8. We ||||||||||||| like Jim.

■ ■ Write these sentences. Use **doesn't** or **don't** to finish each sentence.

1. Carlo and Suzanne ||||||||||||| know the rules.
2. Lester ||||||||||||| either.
3. Ramses ||||||||||||| like canned dog food.
4. The Smiths ||||||||||||| live here.
5. We ||||||||||||| need anything else.
6. Mrs. Enders ||||||||||||| know the answer.
7. Ellen ||||||||||||| know what to do.
8. Bill and José ||||||||||||| want to go.
9. Clara ||||||||||||| swim very well.

Rule 18.

The chart shows five forms of each verb. Use the
verb form that goes with the subject and the time
you want to tell about.

Present Tense		Past Tense	With **Be**	With **Have**
base form	**-s form**	**-ed form**	**-ing form**	**-n form**
like	likes	liked	is liking	has liked
jump	jumps	jumped	is jumping	has jumped
study	studies	studied	is studying	has studied
run	runs	ran	is running	has run
do	does	did	is doing	has done
eat	eats	ate	is eating	has eaten

For Practice

■ Use a form of the verb in the boxes to finish each
sentence. Write the whole sentence.

1. We go to the fair last week.
2. Kyle ride on the roller coaster now.
3. The bus is wait for us.
4. Mrs. Sutro has go home.
5. Darlene sleep until noon last Saturday.
6. The phone was ring .
7. This bus stop in Kalamazoo an hour ago.
8. Letty find three more butterflies yesterday.
9. Millie has help us before.
10. The kitten fall out of the tree yesterday.
11. Cassie was read the newspaper.
12. Russ put another record on the phonograph now.
13. Irene go to the library on Wednesday.
14. Bill is pitch today.
15. Darlene has take her medicine this morning.
16. She pitch the ball very well.

F. DETERMINERS

Rule

Determiners are words that can come before nouns.

> **This car belongs to Ms. Smithers.**
> **That car belongs to Mr. Williams.**

Each word in this box is a **determiner**.

a	this	these	three
an	that	one	some
the	those	two	many

For Practice

■ Find the determiner in the subject of each sentence. Write only the determiner.

1. The light is bright.
2. These books belong here.
3. Two boys joined us.
4. An aardvark has large ears.
5. Those animals are hungry.
6. This box is too small.
7. That window is broken.
8. Many people go to the parade.

■ ■ Find the determiner in the subject of each sentence. Put another determiner in its place. Write the changed sentence.

1. The airplane landed.
2. A noise startled everyone.
3. An animal ran past us.
4. That dog is friendly.
5. Three girls waited there.
6. Some clouds gathered.
7. The rocket blasted off.

G. PRONOUNS

Rule 1.

The words in the box are **pronouns.** A **pronoun** may be used in place of a proper noun or a determiner and noun.

I	**me**
he, she, it	**him, her, it**
we	**us**
they	**them**
you	**you**

These sentences have pronouns in them.

We drove to the next town.
Mr. Green showed us the way.
Laura and he were waiting at the corner.
Michele and I were glad to be there.

For Practice

■ Find the pronoun in each sentence. Write only the pronoun.

1. Janet waited for him at the corner.
2. Jerry put it on the shelf.
3. She ran through the rain.
4. We went to the basketball game.
5. Terry spent the day with us.
6. The man gave them the keys.
7. Tom played handball with me.
8. That package is a present for you.
9. Jim sat next to her.
10. She practices the piano every day.
11. They went to the football game.
12. He picked up the coat.

■ ■ Add a pronoun to each sentence. Write the sentence.

1. Larry threw the ball to ....
2. .... picked up the ball and ran.
3. James put .... on the table.
4. Mother and .... watched television.
5. The man showed .... the way.
6. .... found our sweaters.
7. John helped .... fix the car.
8. .... handed the book to Dad.

Rule 2.

I and **We**; **We** and **Us**

Use **I** and **we** in these sentences.

 I walked to the store.
 We met at the corner.

If you add other names, you still use **I** and **we.**

 Phyllis, Elaine, and I walked to the store.
 Barbara and we met at the corner.

Use **me** and **us** in these sentences.

 Charles greeted me.
 Charles greeted us.

If you add other names, you still use **me** and **us.**

 Charles greeted Scott, Mary, and me.
 Charles greeted Scott and us.

For Practice

■ Write the second sentence in each pair. Use **I** or **me** to finish the sentence.

1. I ran around the track.
   John and ||||||||||||| raced.
2. I rode the bus to school.
   Karen and ||||||||||||| met on it.
3. The rain fell on me.
   It fell on Ted and |||||||||||||.

4. I moved my pawn.
   Carl and ||||||||||||| played chess.
5. He helped me with my homework.
   He explained it to Jane and |||||||||||||.
6. My cousin wrote me a letter.
   Mom read it to Laura and |||||||||||||.

■ ■ Write the second sentence in each pair. Use **we** or **us** to finish the sentence.

1. Michael told us about his trip to Europe.
   He showed the class and ||||||||||||| his souvenirs.
2. We met Lisa and Roger at the dock.
   Lisa, Roger, and ||||||||||||| went sailing.
3. We played touch football with Dick and Marilyn.
   Dick, Marilyn, and ||||||||||||| had a good time.
4. We boarded the airplane with Jill and Henry.
   Jill, Henry, and ||||||||||||| flew to New York.
5. Jane met us at the airport.
   She invited Jill, Henry, and ||||||||||||| to stay with her.
6. Mother took us to a movie.
   She bought popcorn for herself, the twins, and |||||||||||||.

Rule 3.

He and **Him; She** and **Her; They** and **Them**

Use **he, she,** and **they** in these sentences.

> **He climbed the mountain.**
> **She climbed the mountain.**
> **They climbed the mountain.**

If you add other names, you still use **he, she,** and **they.**

> **Keith, Larry, and he climbed the mountain.**
> **Lisa, Polly, and she climbed the mountain.**
> **Nina and they climbed the mountain.**

Use **him, her,** and **them** in these sentences.

> **Other climbers helped him.**
> **Other climbers helped her.**
> **Other climbers helped them.**

If you add other names, you still use **him, her,** and **them.**

> **Other climbers helped Stanley, Barbara, and him.**
> **Other climbers helped Nancy, Greg, and her.**
> **Other climbers helped Darnell and them.**

For Practice

■ Write the second sentence in each pair. Use **he** or **him, she** or **her,** or **they** or **them** to finish each one.

1. Susan asked him to her birthday party.
   She asked Ted and ⦚⦚⦚⦚⦚⦚ to it.
2. They went to the gym.
   Mark and ⦚⦚⦚⦚⦚⦚ played handball.
3. She picked apples.
   Lonny and ⦚⦚⦚⦚⦚⦚ picked a bushelful.
4. He took them to school in the car.
   He took Johnny and ⦚⦚⦚⦚⦚⦚ too.
5. The police officer gave him directions.
   The officer helped Karen and ⦚⦚⦚⦚⦚⦚ .
6. We like hot dogs.
   Larry and ⦚⦚⦚⦚⦚⦚ cooked them.
7. They sailed through the harbor.
   Andrea and ⦚⦚⦚⦚⦚⦚ sailed the boat.

8. He worked with his partner.
   Peter and ⦚⦚⦚⦚⦚⦚ worked together.
9. The coach put her on the first team.
   He put Ron, Dale, and ⦚⦚⦚⦚⦚⦚ on too.
10. They marched in the parade.
    Bryan and ⦚⦚⦚⦚⦚⦚ marched together.
11. The children found him in the library.
    The children found Cara and ⦚⦚⦚⦚⦚⦚ .
12. Dad saved some cake for them.
    Dad saved it for George and ⦚⦚⦚⦚⦚⦚ .
13. We have some candy.
    Tina and ⦚⦚⦚⦚⦚⦚ eat the candy.
14. We looked for them.
    We found David, Tina, and ⦚⦚⦚⦚⦚⦚ .

Rule 4.

The words in the box are **possessive pronouns.**
Pronouns in this form show ownership.

my	**your**	**his**	**her**	**its**	**our**	**their**

For Practice

■ Find the possessive pronoun in each sentence.
Write just that word.

1. Chris left his notebook at home.
2. The little kitten misses its mother.
3. Is this your watch?
4. Bessie took our picture.
5. I signed my name at the bottom.
6. Elena is their sister.
7. My brother works there.
8. Charlotte explained her idea.
9. They closed our school early.
10. Her cat is called Sandy.

■ ■ Add a different possessive pronoun to each
sentence. Write the whole sentence.

1. Tanya wrote to .... pen pal.
2. Steve lent Tina .... baseball mitt.
3. We slept in .... tents.
4. Our bird stays in .... cage.
5. The dogs wagged .... tails.
6. I like .... sister.
7. .... brother fixed the leak.
8. The snake shed .... skin.
9. .... books are in the locker.
10. We borrowed .... paint sets.
11. Paula likes .... horse.
12. When will .... meal be ready?

Rule 5.

The words in the box are **indefinite pronouns.**

anybody	**everybody**	**somebody**	**nobody**
anyone	**everyone**	**someone**	**no one**
anything	**everything**	**something**	**nothing**

For Practice

■ Find the indefinite pronoun in each sentence.
Write only the indefinite pronoun.

1. Everything seems funny today.
2. Anyone could have done it.
3. No one was there.
4. Nothing helps.
5. Something is wrong.
6. Everyone spoke at once.
7. Nobody laughed at my joke.
8. Someone will help us.
9. I have spoken to everybody.
10. Anybody can help.

■■ Add a different indefinite pronoun to each
sentence. Write the whole sentence.

1. .... called.
2. .... happened.
3. .... told a joke.
4. .... surprises me.
5. .... knows that secret.
6. .... likes Jason.
7. .... could do it.
8. .... knocked.
9. .... listened.
10. .... caught the ball.
11. .... picked the flowers.
12. .... worked all night.

Rule 6.

An **indefinite pronoun** can be the subject of a sentence. When it is, use the verb form that goes with singular subjects.

Everyone stops.
Nothing happens.

For Practice

■ The subject of each of these sentences is an indefinite pronoun. Use the correct verb form to finish each sentence. Write the sentence.

1. Everybody   ice cream. (like, likes)
2. Someone   on the door. (knocks, knock)
3. Everything   at once. (happen, happens)
4. No one   the answer. (know, knows)
5. Anything   with milk. (goes, go)
6. Something   wrong. (seems, seem)
7. Nothing   . (change, changes)
8. Anyone   a chance. (has, have)
9. Everyone   . (laugh, laughs)
10. Somebody   us. (helps, help)
11. Everybody   an opinion. (have, has)
12. Nobody   that road. (use, uses)
13. Nothing   Natalie. (bothers, bother)
14. Everything   . (change, changes)
15. Someone   every game. (wins, win)
16. No one   here. (work, works)
17. Someone   to my requests. (listen, listens)
18. Something   into the well. (fall, falls)
19. Nobody   her call. (hear, hears)
20. Anybody   him. (visit, visits)
21. Everyone   today. (play, plays)
22. Anything   with it. (blend, blends)

H. ADJECTIVES

Rule 1.

Use the sentence in the box to test for adjectives.
Any word that fits in the blank can be an adjective.

> **That is very** ⦙⦙⦙⦙⦙⦙⦙⦙⦙ .

That is very pretty .   **adjective**
That is very flower .   **not an adjective**

For Practice

■ Use the test sentence to check these words. Write
only the adjectives.

1. good	7. train	13. delicate
2. work	8. little	14. big
3. large	9. red	15. car
4. street	10. soft	16. yellow
5. tall	11. pencil	17. fresh
6. house	12. tablet	18. beautiful

■■ Find the adjective in the predicate of each
sentence. Write only the adjectives.

1. The truck is big.
2. The soup smells good.
3. The water in the pan feels hot.
4. The soup tastes delicious.

5. This plant stays green all year.
6. The baby remained quiet.
7. Your plans are excellent.
8. The joke was funny.

■■■ Add an adjective to the subject of each
sentence. Write the sentence.

1. The ⦙⦙⦙⦙⦙⦙⦙ stream has many fish in it.
2. The ⦙⦙⦙⦙⦙⦙⦙ puppy wagged its tail.
3. Many ⦙⦙⦙⦙⦙⦙⦙ pictures were on display.
4. Three ⦙⦙⦙⦙⦙⦙⦙ boys played in the yard.
5. The ⦙⦙⦙⦙⦙⦙⦙ car rolled to a stop.

6. A ⦙⦙⦙⦙⦙⦙⦙ fox ran after the rabbit.
7. A ⦙⦙⦙⦙⦙⦙⦙ storm broke out.
8. The ⦙⦙⦙⦙⦙⦙⦙ flower is blooming.
9. His ⦙⦙⦙⦙⦙⦙⦙ shirt was torn.
10. ⦙⦙⦙⦙⦙⦙⦙ trees grew along the road.

Rule 2.

Add **-er** to an adjective when you compare two people or things. Add **-est** to an adjective when you compare more than two people or things.

Lisa is tall.
Mike is taller than Lisa.
Shelley is the tallest of all.

For Practice

■ Write each sentence. If the sentence compares two people or things, add **-er** to the adjective in the box. If the sentence compares more than two people or things, add **-est** to the adjective in the box.

1. This building is `old` than that one.
2. The building on the corner is the `old` one of all.
3. Wally is the `young` of three children.
4. An orange is `sweet` than a grapefruit.
5. This book is `long` than that one.
6. The big package is `light` than the small one.
7. We climbed the `high` mountain in the area.
8. We chose the `small` kitten of the seven.
9. Clem is the `silly` clown of all.
10. Your bike goes `fast` than mine.
11. This lake is `long` than that one.
12. It is the `long` lake in the state.
13. She dove `deep` than Bettina.
14. Marc made the `deep` dive of the day.
15. What is the `fast` animal in the world?
16. This is the `short` day of the year.
17. Sunday was `hot` than Tuesday.
18. The seashore is the `cool` place to be.
19. That room is `damp` than this one.
20. We sat in the `dark` room in the house.

Rule 3.

Use **more** or **most** before some adjectives in comparisons. Use **more** when you compare two people or things. Use **most** when you compare more than two people or things.

Jeff's story was humorous.
Pietro's story was more humorous than Jeff's.
Nancy's story was the most humorous of all.

For Practice

■ Write each sentence. If the sentence is about two people or things, use **more** before the adjective in the box. If the sentence is about more than two people or things, use **most** before the adjective.

1. Cory's painting is colorful than mine.
2. Leslie painted the colorful picture in the show.
3. This ten-speed bike is expensive than the other one.
4. Dasher is the awkward puppy in the litter.
5. The living room is pleasant than the attic.
6. Bruce is the graceful player on the team.
7. Marlene has the wonderful news of all.
8. The young pony is active than our old horse.
9. Bonnie is the curious member of our family.
10. Ms. Okino is the careful driver I know.
11. That was the enjoyable show we had ever seen.
12. Gary was helpful than his sister.
13. Rodney is the thoughtful boy in the class.
14. She is the forgetful person in town.
15. This dictionary is useful than that one.
16. This is the interesting picture of all.
17. Our toys were colorful than their toys.
18. This is the ancient book of them all.
19. I think the moon is beautiful than the sun.
20. I am careless than she is.

Rule 4.

Use **good** or **bad** when you tell about one thing.
Use **better** or **worse** when you compare two things.
Use **best** or **worst** when you compare three or
more things.

This book is good.
It is better than the last book I read.
It is the best book I have ever read.
This television show is bad.
It is worse than the Saturday morning
show.
It is the worst show I have ever seen.

For Practice

■ Write these sentences. Use **good, better,** or **best**
to finish each sentence.

1. We fixed a ||||||||||||| dinner.
2. Sharon is the ||||||||||||| guard on the team.
3. Mark's drawing is ||||||||||||| than the one in the book.
4. Our new car is ||||||||||||| than the old one.
5. Highway 17 is the ||||||||||||| route to Centerville.
6. We saw a ||||||||||||| movie.
7. This is the ||||||||||||| book.
8. This car is the ||||||||||||| car we have ever owned.

■ ■ Write these sentences. Use **bad, worse,** or
worst to finish each sentence.

1. A ||||||||||||| storm broke out in the afternoon.
2. This is the ||||||||||||| cold I have ever had.
3. Our team played its ||||||||||||| game of the season.
4. A rainy day is a ||||||||||||| day for a picnic.
5. Skipping breakfast is ||||||||||||| than going without lunch.
6. A toothache can be ||||||||||||| than a headache.
7. This is the ||||||||||||| snowstorm of the season.
8. Our new plan is ||||||||||||| than the old one.

Rule 5.

A **completer** is a word or a group of words that follows a form of **be.** A completer may be an **adjective.**

The story was funny.

For Practice

■ The verb in each of these sentences is a form of **be.** Write the adjective completer from each sentence.

1. Therese is happy.
2. The baby is curious.
3. The guests were hungry.
4. The animals are graceful.
5. The students are interested.
6. The room was crowded.
7. This closet is empty.
8. The movie was boring.
9. Ben was sad.
10. The bird is tiny.
11. Mrs. Jeffers is busy.
12. We were tired.
13. The meeting was long.
14. The people were asleep.
15. The puppy is healthy.
16. Those cars are big.
17. Our dinner was cold.
18. The shelves were dusty.
19. Our breakfast was delicious.
20. The seals are playful.
21. The ground was wet.
22. His job was funny.

■■ Write three sentences. Use a form of **be** and an adjective completer in each one.

I. ADVERBS

Rule

Adverbs are words that tell **how, when,** or **where.**
Read these sentences. The words in color are **adverbs.**

The men worked carefully.
The plane takes off tomorrow.
The children played indoors.

For Practice

■ Find the adverbs in these sentences. Write only
the adverbs.

1. The dog barked loudly.
2. The play opens tomorrow.
3. Everyone rushed outside.
4. This rain started yesterday.
5. He whistled softly.
6. Everyone met here.
7. Flowers bloomed everywhere.
8. The boys waited silently.
9. The package arrived today.
10. The girls smiled politely.

■ ■ Add an adverb from the box to each sentence.
Write the sentence.

1. The boys walked ||||||||||||||.
2. We will meet ||||||||||||||.
3. The cork fits ||||||||||||||.
4. The club met ||||||||||||||.
5. He drew the map ||||||||||||||.
6. The turtle moved ||||||||||||||.
7. The play begins |||||||||||||| at 8:00 P.M.
8. She shouted ||||||||||||||.
9. We left ||||||||||||||.
10. They left their books ||||||||||||||.

bravely	outside
carefully	quickly
easily	slowly
neatly	loudly
here	tomorrow
inside	tonight
now	yesterday

J. PREPOSITIONS

Rule 1.

Some sentences have prepositions. Each word in
the box is a preposition.

above	before	during	in	off	through	with
after	below	for	into	on	to	without
at	by	from	of	over	under	behind

For Practice

■ Find the preposition in each of these sentences.
Write just the preposition.

1. Jed waited on the corner.
2. Everyone dove into the pool.
3. Your friends are waiting for you.
4. Judy climbed to the top.
5. Zev left with his mother.
6. The plane flew above the clouds.
7. Sam fell asleep during the movie.
8. We put our lunches in the knapsack.
9. Greta moved to Kansas.
10. She lives on a farm.
11. The train left without me.
12. The dog hid under the stairs.
13. He dove from the high board.
14. That road goes through town.
15. The sun rises over the hill.
16. Clara met me at the store.
17. The sun set behind the hill.
18. He left it in the closet.
19. The book is signed by the author.
20. The hikers can be found below the cliff.

Rule 2.

A preposition may be followed by a determiner and a noun. The preposition, the determiner, and the noun are called a **prepositional phrase.**

Art went to the movies.

A preposition may be followed by a proper noun. The preposition and the proper noun are called a **prepositional phrase.**

Kim went with Art.

For Practice

■ Find the prepositional phrases in the sentences below. Write each prepositional phrase.

1. We hiked through the forest.
2. Nola lives in that building.
3. Dawn received a postcard from Wanda.
4. Miss Brodsky is the coach of the team.
5. The team practices in the park.
6. Claire passed the ball to Rodney.
7. I left the book on that chair.
8. This plane flies from Omaha.

■ ■ Add a preposition to each of these sentences. Write the sentences.

1. This bus goes ||||||||||||| Centerville.
2. Joel left his shoes ||||||||||||| the bed.
3. Jamie waited ||||||||||||| Mrs. McIntyre.
4. Everyone laughed ||||||||||||| the movie.
5. Lorie planted the garden ||||||||||||| the house.
6. The letter is ||||||||||||| Martha.
7. My paper is ||||||||||||| the book.
8. The kitten is ||||||||||||| the box.
9. The class was ||||||||||||| the gym.
10. They climbed ||||||||||||| the cave.

Rule 3.

A preposition may be followed by one of the pronouns in the box. The preposition and the pronoun are called a **prepositional phrase.**

me	**you**	**him**	**her**	**it**	**us**	**them**

Dr. Conway spoke to us.

For Practice

■ Each of these sentences has a preposition followed by a pronoun. Write the prepositional phrase from each sentence.

1. Mavis waved to them.
2. I borrowed the book from him.
3. The puppy ran after us.
4. Stan saved a place for me.
5. Did Colleen go with you?
6. Bill took a picture of her.
7. Maurie keeps the tools in it.
8. Mr. Fracchia discussed his ideas with us.
9. I took it from them.
10. Paul selected the fruit for us.

■■ Add a pronoun to finish the prepositional phrase in each sentence. Write the sentences.

1. Kip waited for ||||||||||||||.
2. I have a note from ||||||||||||||.
3. Mom gave the money to ||||||||||||||.
4. Dr. Ostrum went with ||||||||||||||.
5. Moira left without ||||||||||||||.
6. Karl sang for ||||||||||||||.
7. We like cleaning up for ||||||||||||||.
8. We have a portrait of ||||||||||||||.
9. Let us go to ||||||||||||||.

Rule 4.

A completer is a word or a group of words that
follows a form of **be.** A **prepositional phrase** may
be a completer.

Mona is in the garden
Her friends are with her.

For Practice

■ The completers in these sentences are
prepositional phrases. Write the completer from
each sentence.

1. Craig and Tandy are in the kitchen.
2. Dinner is on the stove.
3. The cabin is in the woods.
4. Seven boats were on the lake.
5. The letters were from Aunt Rose.
6. They were for me.
7. The answers are in the book.
8. The suitcases are in the basement.
9. The sailors are with the captain.
10. Our crew is on the deck.

■ ■ Add a prepositional phrase completer to each
sentence. Write the whole sentence.

1. Molly is   .
2. The baby's toys are   .
3. The fruit is   .
4. Dr. Dwan is   .
5. Nicolas was   .
6. The boats are   .
7. The garden is   .
8. Their class is   .
9. Our books are   .
10. The seals were   .

Rule 5.

A **prepositional phrase** may be part of the subject of a sentence. The words in color are prepositional phrases.

The book on the table **is mine.**
The stories in that book **are funny.**

For Practice

■ Find the prepositional phrase in the subject of each sentence. Write just the prepositional phrase.

1. The girls with Juanita are her sisters.
2. The bridge over that river should be repaired.
3. The people at the party were friendly.
4. The clothes in the washer are clean now.
5. The toys under the table are the dog's.
6. The patient before me seemed nervous.
7. The bird in this cage is a cockatoo.
8. The phone call during the night surprised us.
9. The children below the cliff are tired.
10. The statues on the shelf need dusting.

■ ■ Add a prepositional phrase to the subject of each sentence. Write the whole sentence.

1. The clock   is slow.
2. The girl   is Consuelo.
3. The books   are Scott's.
4. The room   is the living room.
5. The path   is narrow.
6. The pictures   are pretty.
7. The boy   is Tonio.
8. The books   are old.
9. The blocks   need to be cut.
10. The children   are having fun.
11. The noise   sounded strange.
12. The ghost   scared them.

Rule 6.

When you add a **prepositional phrase** to the subject of a sentence, you do not change the form of the verb.

> **The book is heavy.**
> **The book on the shelf is heavy.**
>
> **The books are heavy.**
> **The books on the shelf are heavy.**

For Practice

■ Find the verb in the predicate. Write just the verb.

1. The dogs in the yard are noisy.
2. The girl from India likes Los Angeles.
3. The plane below the clouds is a jet.
4. The book on top is mine.
5. The road through town is narrow.
6. The lunches in the basket seem stale.
7. The teachers with the class are Ms. Levin and Mr. Thorpe.
8. The tunnel through the mountain is not safe.

■■ Add a verb to each sentence. Write the sentence.

1. The girls in the class |||||||||||| quiet.
2. The view from the mountain |||||||||||| beautiful.
3. The hat under the stairs |||||||||||| John's.
4. The man behind the desk |||||||||||| busy.
5. The sounds during the night |||||||||||| scary.
6. The curtains on the window |||||||||||| dirty.
7. The road into the mountains |||||||||||| winding.
8. The ball and bat on the shelf |||||||||||| Amy's.
9. The creature in the forest |||||||||||| huge.
10. The noise from the street |||||||||||| deafening.
11. The party on the ship |||||||||||| fun.
12. Parties on ships |||||||||||| fun.

K. CONJUNCTIONS

Rule

The words in the box are **conjunctions.** You can
use a conjunction to join two sentences in a
compound sentence.

and   but   or

The bell rang, and everyone left the room.
The bell rang, but no one left the room.
We can wait for the bell, or we can leave now.

For Practice

■ Use a conjunction to join the two sentences in
each pair. Write the compound sentences you make.

1. Melba watched television. Maurice read the newspaper.
2. We'll have to hurry. We'll be late.
3. Dale peeled the potatoes. Bud cut up the carrots.
4. Tony asked for a hamburger. The waitress brought
   him a hot dog.
5. Mrs. David rides the bus. Miss Blandon rides in
   a carpool.
6. Sidney played the guitar. Everyone sang along.
7. Juanita raised her hand. The teacher called on her.
8. I know we have an extra key. I don't know where it is.
9. The score was tied. There were only two
   minutes left.
10. You can come with us. You can wait here.
11. Stacy will pitch today. Henry will pitch tomorrow.
12. The clock is slow. The watch is fast.
13. The snow is falling. The heat melts it.
14. The arrow hit the target. She won a prize.
15. I left the party. I came back later.
16. We found the money. We gave it back.

L. SUBORDINATORS

Rule 1.

The words in the box are **subordinators.** You can use a subordinator to join two sentences in a new sentence.

after before when whenever while

Everyone clapped when the play was over.
The actors bowed while the audience applauded.

For Practice

■ Find the subordinator in each sentence. Write just the subordinator.

1. Our dog barks whenever someone rings the doorbell.
2. I washed the dishes while you watched television.
3. Janet runs a mile each day before she goes to school.
4. Nate wants to travel after he finishes school.
5. Betty wasn't home when I called.
6. Daisy listens to the radio while she has breakfast.
7. I have to finish this project before I can start a new one.
8. Neda took pictures of us while we worked.

■ ■ Use a subordinator from the box to combine the sentences in each pair. Write the sentences you make.

1. Burt took a shower. He went swimming.
2. Doug went to sleep. He watched his favorite television show.
3. Everyone stopped working. The bell rang.
4. The cat hides. The dog comes into the house.
5. Jake always yells. The Cougars score.
6. We visit the museum. We are in the city.
7. Scot mowed the lawn. He played ball.
8. Lucinda read her book. She waited for her mother.

Rule 2.

The words in the box are **subordinators.** You can use a subordinator to join two sentences in a new sentence.

| **although** | **because** | **if** | **though** | **unless** |

I'll try this if you will.
I won't try this unless you do.

For Practice

■ Find the subordinator in each sentence. Write just the subordinator.

1. We shouldn't go skating unless the ice is safe.
2. Raul overslept because his alarm did not ring.
3. No one laughed although the story was funny.
4. You should stop in Denver if you have time.
5. Jill did not find any hidden treasure though she followed the directions carefully.
6. Our team will be in first place if we win this game.
7. Dora and Klaus could not play tennis because the courts were wet.
8. The train won't leave unless everyone is on board.

■ ■ Use a subordinator from the box to combine the sentences in each pair. Write the new sentences.

1. Nick may not watch television tonight. He has too much homework.
2. My little brother played outside. It was raining.
3. Andrea enjoyed the book. The characters were funny.
4. We'll go on a picnic. The weather is good.
5. You can win the game. You make the right move now.
6. Nancy went to the party. Her brother stayed home.
7. He won't do the job. We help him.

M. RELATIVE CLAUSES WITH **WHO, WHICH,** AND **THAT**

Rule 1.

You can sometimes use the word **who** to join two
sentences about people to make a new sentence.

> **We met the doctor.**
> **The doctor performed the operation.**
> **We met the doctor who performed the operation.**

For Practice

■ Use the word **who** to join the sentences in each
pair. Write the sentences you make.

1. I like the people. The people helped us.
2. The letter came from my cousin. My cousin
   lives in Rio de Janeiro.
3. Mr. Lee thanked the boys. The boys cleaned
   the basement.
4. The president introduced the doctor. The doctor
   spoke to the science club.
5. Laverne knows the woman. A woman trains
   circus animals.
6. Dr. Bost is the dentist. The dentist takes care
   of our teeth.
7. Mr. Vandon is the teacher. The teacher led the
   field trip.
8. The police have found the child. The child was lost.
9. We asked the librarian. The librarian had helped
   us before.
10. Sally waved to the girls. The girls were leaving.
11. My brother is the boy. My brother washes the car
    every Saturday.
12. Tanya shops with someone. Someone knows all
    the good shops.

Rule 2.

You can sometimes use the word **which** to join two sentences about animals or things to make a new sentence.

We're waiting for the train.
The train goes to Seattle.
We're waiting for the train which goes to Seattle.

For Practice

▪ Use the word **which** to join the sentences in each pair. Write the sentences you make.

1. Molly goes to the school. The school is near her house.
2. Darryl trained the dog. The dog can jump through a hoop.
3. Corliss watered the plants. The plants looked dry.
4. Someone took the bikes. The bikes were leaning against the house.
5. We fished from the bridge. The bridge goes across the river.
6. Jenny sewed on the buttons. The buttons had fallen off.
7. Lenny opened the trunk. The trunk was in the attic.
8. Mrs. Karensky explained the question. The question had confused us.
9. Mom and Dad want to see the movie. The movie is showing at the Pick Theater.
10. The gardener pruned the trees. The trees had grown too big.
11. The dog grabbed the bone. The bone was on the table.
12. We found the treasure. The treasure was in the attic.
13. The table was filled with food. The food was very good to look at.

Rule 3.

You can sometimes use the word **that** to join two sentences about people, animals, or things to make a new sentence.

> **We heard the plane.**
> **The plane flew overhead.**
> **We heard the plane that flew overhead.**
>
> **We saw the pilot.**
> **The pilot parachuted from the plane.**
> **We saw the pilot that parachuted from the plane.**

For Practice

■ Use the word **that** to join the sentences in each pair. Write the sentences you make.

1. Rick chose the puppy. The puppy bit his finger.
2. Mom is looking for the books. The books are due at the library.
3. Chrissie helped the workers. The workers were repairing the fence.
4. Wendy will like the gift. The gift is in this box.
5. Someone threw away the bottles. The bottles were in the closet.
6. We're looking for an island. An island isn't on the map.
7. Ice is water. Water has frozen.
8. Will knows the wranglers. The wranglers work on Mr. Valenti's ranch.
9. Ray enjoys television shows. Television shows make him laugh.
10. Everyone watched the clouds. The clouds darkened the sky.
11. We climbed the hill. The hill was very steep.
12. They saw the strange animal. The strange animal was coming out of the cave.

PART 3
Choosing the Right Word

N. A AND AN

Rule

Use **a** before words that begin with consonant sounds.

a ball   **a pig**

Use **an** before words that begin with vowel sounds.

an aardvark   **an elf**   **an endless road**

For Practice

■ Write these sentences. Use **a** or **an** to finish each.

1. Jerry watched _____ ant crawl into the sand.
2. The boy picked up _____ leaf.
3. Mary found _____ unusual shell.
4. Larry rode _____ elephant in the circus parade.
5. The squirrel jumped from the branch of ~~an~~ oak tree.
6. Water dripped from _____ icicle.
7. Karen wrote _____ interesting letter to her friend.
8. Bruce peeled _____ orange.
9. We went to _____ restaurant on Fourth Street.
10. Ted cooked _____ eggplant.
11. They could see _____ light in the house.
12. Susan lit _____ candle.
13. Is that _____ eagle?
14. No, it is _____ hawk.
15. _____ iceberg can be very big.
16. What is the difference between _____ oyster and _____ clam?
17. I bought _____ book and _____ ice cream cone.
18. We have _____ large cat in our house.

O. **TO, TOO,** AND **TWO**

Rule

Use **to** in sentences such as these.

> **Ben walked to the store.**
> **He planned to buy a sweater.**

Use **too** in sentences such as these.

> **His car is new too.**
> **The car is too big.**

Use **two** in sentences such as this.

> **The two boys walked home.**

For Practice

■ Write these sentences. Use **to, too,** or **two** to finish each sentence.

1. The girls like ||||||||||||| fish.
2. Everyone wanted ||||||||||||| win the prize.
3. She waved at the ||||||||||||| boys.
4. Ned put ||||||||||||| books on the library shelf.
5. We live on Central Street |||||||||||||.
6. ||||||||||||| students worked on this science project.
7. The mountains are ||||||||||||| far away for a weekend trip.
8. We will go ||||||||||||| the mountains on our vacation.
9. Les handed the sales clerk ||||||||||||| coins.
10. Lila rides her bicycle ||||||||||||| school each day.
11. Mark wants to go with us |||||||||||||.
12. The box is ||||||||||||| heavy.
13. We have ||||||||||||| books ||||||||||||| bring back.
14. I ate ||||||||||||| much salad.
15. We are going ||||||||||||| the pool |||||||||||||.
16. May I swim |||||||||||||?
17. Please feed the ||||||||||||| cats.

P. **TEACH** AND **LEARN**

Rule

Use a form of **teach** when you mean "to instruct a person or animal."

> **Denise teaches children to swim.**
> **She taught my brother to do the backstroke.**

Use a form of **learn** when you mean "to gain a skill or knowledge."

> **The children learn about water safety.**
> **My brother learned to do the backstroke.**

For Practice

■ Finish each sentence. Use **teach, teaches, taught, learn, learns,** or **learned.** Write the sentence.

1. Mr. Wang ⬚⬚⬚⬚ our art class every Thursday.
2. We ⬚⬚⬚⬚ how to mix paints.
3. Joe ⬚⬚⬚⬚ his dog tricks last year.
4. His dog ⬚⬚⬚⬚ easily.
5. Cats can ⬚⬚⬚⬚ tricks too.
6. Donna wants to ⬚⬚⬚⬚ to play tennis.
7. Barbie is going to ⬚⬚⬚⬚ her to play.
8. Miss Maxwell ⬚⬚⬚⬚ our class last year.
9. Bob ⬚⬚⬚⬚ us a new song.
10. I ⬚⬚⬚⬚ to skate last year.
11. They have all ⬚⬚⬚⬚ the new game.
12. Will you ⬚⬚⬚⬚ her to swim?
13. It is hard to ⬚⬚⬚⬚ my cat.
14. Please ⬚⬚⬚⬚ me to throw a curve ball.
15. Joe has ⬚⬚⬚⬚ to speak French.
16. Tomorrow we will be ⬚⬚⬚⬚ in the gym.

■ ■ Write two sentences. Use a different form of **teach** in each sentence. Write two sentences. Use a different form of **learn** in each sentence.

Q. LET AND LEAVE

Rule

Use a form of **let** when you mean "to allow."

> **Let me help you.**
> **Will your mother let you go?**

Use a form of **leave** when you mean "to go away from" or "to allow to remain."

> **We should leave now.**
> **Mona has left for school already.**

For Practice

■ Finish each sentence. Use **let, lets, leave, leaves,** or **left.** Write the sentence.

1. Where did you ⬚⬚⬚ your books?
2. Dad ⬚⬚⬚ me use his desk.
3. I ⬚⬚⬚ my shoes in the gym.
4. Craig has ⬚⬚⬚ for home already.
5. Hope ⬚⬚⬚ her sister borrow her skates.
6. You should ⬚⬚⬚ Jason go with you.
7. What time did they ⬚⬚⬚?
8. Ms. Maxwell ⬚⬚⬚ me sail the boat.
9. Everyone ⬚⬚⬚ the room.
10. The helicopter will ⬚⬚⬚ in ten minutes.
11. ⬚⬚⬚ us go to the museum.
12. We have ⬚⬚⬚ school for the day.
13. Tina ⬚⬚⬚ her glasses on the table.
14. They will ⬚⬚⬚ at dawn.
15. This is a good time to ⬚⬚⬚ the house.
16. The girls did not want to ⬚⬚⬚
17. Our bus has ⬚⬚⬚ the school grounds.
18. ⬚⬚⬚ the dog out for some exercise.

■ ■ Write two sentences using a form of **let.** Write two more sentences. Use a different form of **leave** in each.

R. **SIT** AND **SET**

Rule

Use a form of **sit** when you mean "to rest in a seated position."

We can sit on the couch.
They sat on the floor.

Use a form of **set** when you mean "to put something."

Buddy sets the boxes down here.
Martha set the plant on the ledge.

For Practice

■ Finish each sentence. Use **sit, sits, sat, set,** or **sets.** Write the sentence.

1. The children   on the swings yesterday.
2. Alex   the carton down with a thump.
3. Please   in this chair.
4.   the suitcase down here.
5. Mom always likes to   here.
6. The picnickers   on the grass.
7. Darcy   the books on the top shelf.
8. Where did you   that can?
9. Our dog is learning to   up.
10. We   the plates on the table.
11. They   in the car.
12. May I   next to you?
13. She carefully   down the statue.
14. We have   here for a long time.
15. The children   the boxes over there.
16. I like to   in that chair.

■ ■ Write two sentences. Use a different form of **sit** in each. Write two more sentences. Use a different form of **set** in each.

PART 4

Special Forms

S. FRIENDLY LETTER

Rule

A friendly letter has five parts. Read this letter. Then read the words in color about each part.

date Notice the comma after the number of the day

greeting The greeting ends with a comma.

body The body gives the message of the letter.

name The name tells who wrote the letter.

closing The closing ends with a comma.

> July 18, 1980
>
> Dear Aunt Mary,
>
>   Thank you for having me at your house last week. I really had a good time! It was a lot of fun to go to a concert. I liked the hockey game too.
>
>   I'm at home now. Things seem rather dull around here, but maybe something will happen soon. School will be starting in two weeks. Then I will have plenty to do.
>
>   Love,
>
>   Paul

For Practice

■ Put the parts of this letter in order. Then write the letter.

1. Dear Kay,
2. Alice
3. August 10, 1980
4. As ever,

5.   How nice it was to hear from you! Thank you for writing. It sounds like you're having a good summer.

   I haven't decided just how I will spend the rest of the summer. I'm thinking about visiting my cousins in Chicago. Have you ever been there?

■ ■ Pretend that you are making plans for the summer. Write a letter to a friend. Tell the friend about your plans.

T. BUSINESS LETTER

Rule

A business letter has six parts. Read this letter.
Then read the words in color naming each part.

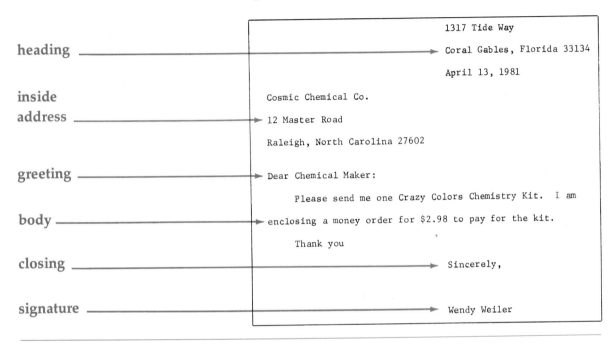

heading

    1317 Tide Way
    Coral Gables, Florida 33134
    April 13, 1981

inside address

    Cosmic Chemical Co.
    12 Master Road
    Raleigh, North Carolina 27602

greeting

    Dear Chemical Maker:

body

        Please send me one Crazy Colors Chemistry Kit. I am
    enclosing a money order for $2.98 to pay for the kit.
        Thank you

closing

                        Sincerely,

signature

                        Wendy Weiler

For Practice

■ Put the parts of this business letter in order.
Write the whole letter.

1. Dear Magic Show Maker:
2. 202 Central Boulevard
   Holland, Michigan 49423
   December 13, 1980
3. Merry Magic, Inc.
   1444 Benson Street
   Amarillo, Texas 79109
4. Tommy Chang
5. Sincerely,
6.   On November 1, 1980, I ordered
   a Magic Show from you. I sent a
   money order for $4.50. The Magic
   Show, however, has not arrived.
   Please send it as soon as possible.

■ ■ Think of something you would like. Write a
business letter ordering it.

U. ENVELOPES

Rule

An envelope has two parts. Read the envelope and
the words in color.

```
Ann Sanders

4812 Prospect Avenue

Kalamazoo, Michigan 49008




                              John Dinoli

                              3617 Pleasant Drive

                              Lansing, Michigan 48910
```

return address
The return address
tells where the letter
is coming from. The
return address has a
name, street, city,
state, and zip code.

address
The address tells where the
letter is going. The address
has a name, street, city,
state, and zip code.

For Practice

■ Show how you would address these envelopes.

From
Joe Valasquez
1124 Waverly Drive
Gary, Indiana 46410

To
James Brooks
1418 Cedar Street
Decatur, Illinois 62516

From
Elizabeth Parker
3340 Pine Street
Springfield, Missouri 65804

To
Lea Goldberg
1813 Elm Street
Abilene, Kansas 67410

From
Dale Ellis
2617 Canton Avenue
Boston, Massachusetts 02118

To
Paul Howard
1134 Charles Street
New Rochelle, New York 10805

V. OUTLINES

Rule

Outlines are plans for writing. Outlines list the ideas you want to put in your story. Outlines show these ideas in order. The main ideas in an outline have Roman numerals. Other ideas have capital letters.

The outline below shows a plan for writing a paper about hurricanes.

Hurricanes

I. The Hurricane Develops
   A. Water Vapor
   B. Wind Spiral
   C. Water Condensation

II. The Hurricane Travels
   A. Speed
   B. Direction

III. The Hurricane Strikes
   A. Warning Clouds
   B. Wind and Rain
   C. "Eye" of the Storm
   D. Return of Wind and Rain

For Practice

■ Look at the outline. Read the main ideas. Then look at the other ideas below. Decide which two ideas belong under each main idea. Then write the whole outline.

Where to Plant	Judging Ripeness
Watering	When to Plant
Weeding	Time of Day to Harvest

■ ■ Write an outline for one of these titles. Put at least three main ideas in your outline. Put two other ideas under each main idea.

Giving a Party	Healthful Eating
Choosing a Summer Camp	Making a |||||||||||||
Modern Transportation	

Growing Vegetables

I. Planting the Vegetables
   A.
   B.
II. Caring for the Plants
   A.
   B.
III. Harvesting the Vegetables
   A.
   B.

W. PARAGRAPHS

Rule

A paragraph is a group of sentences that tells about one thing. The first line of a paragraph is indented. It begins farther from the left edge of the paper than the other lines.

    Minstrels were poets and musicians who wandered through Europe in the Middle Ages. Minstrels entertained the people. They sang songs and recited poems. Minstrels made up stories to tell. Other minstrels repeated old ballads and folk tales. The stories of some minstrels are still remembered today.

For Practice

■ Read each group of sentences. Decide which group has sentences that all tell about the same thing. Write that group of sentences as a paragraph. Remember to indent the first sentence.

Group 1

Dolphins are interesting, entertaining animals. They swim swiftly and gracefully. They are also very intelligent. This combination makes the dolphin a good performer. Many dolphins have been trained to perform tricks and entertain.

Group 2

Much of our sugar comes from sugar cane. This is a tall grass plant that grows in tropical and semitropical climates. The stalks of the sugar cane plant are cut and shredded. Then the sweet juice is pressed out of the cane. Honey is also very sweet. The cane juice is made into the sugar we use. Salt is not sweet but it looks like sugar.

Index